CW00927863

The case for the animal is the case of the woman. What is more likely to impress mankind with the necessity of justice for women than the awakening of the idea that justice was the right of even an ox or a sheep.

Edith Ward: *Shafts*

Albatross

There is no denying that slavery had a direct and positive tendency to produce coarseness and brutality in the treatment of animals, especially those most useful to agricultural industry. Not only the slave, but the horse, the ox and the mule shared the general feeling of indifference to the rights naturally engendered by a state of slavery. The master blamed the overseer, the overseer the slave, and the slave the horses, the oxen and mules, and violence fell upon the animals as a consequence.

Frederick Douglass

Albatross

An Anthology of Animal Rights Poetry

Noël Sweeney

This edition was first published in Great Britain in 2024
by Alibi an imprint of Veritas Chambers
Unit 4 + 1 BP Bristol

Copyright © 2024 by Noël Sweeney

The moral right of the author has been asserted in accordance
with the Copyright, Designs and Patents Act 1988.

A catalogue record for this book is available from the British Library.

ISBN 978-1-872724-42-3

Dedication

For Maureen and Wendy and Polly and Pop who were present at the start and still there at the end. They knew buttered parsnips cut no mustard.

What appeal *can* be made to people whose first instinct, on seeing a beautiful animal, full of joyousness and vitality, is to hunt or eat it?

Henry Salt

Acknowledgements

I owe a defined debt to too many to mention each one. Within those truth-tellers are Blake and Clare and Marvell whose spell seeps through the pages serving to prove a purpose worth pursuing. Equally along with them Oliver takes the biscuit.

Those whose sparks struck starlight even on the darkest night are Samuel Sharpe and Martha White.

The vision of Frederick Douglass and Lewis Gompertz and Henry Salt and Isaac Bashevis Singer opened my eyes to a due North moral compass of compassion whose points fixed on the roots of justice and truth.

Helen Jones, Tom Regan and Steven Wise raised their voices to speak for those forever stricken with lockjaw. Beating in time with their footsteps yet primed across the beat is the prescience of Henry Holzer.

Each showed neither fear nor favour nor falsehood in their quest to lessen the plight of all animals.

Also by Noël Sweeney

Animals-in-Law

Dogs of Law

A Practical Approach to Animal Welfare Law

Bees-at-Law

Doris and the Grumpy Judge

English Hungers

An Animals' Charter

In Defence of Bees

Blue-bird sings the Blues

Jungle Judge Justice

I am in favour of animal rights as well as human rights. That is the way of a whole human being.

I care not much for a man's religion whose dog and cat are not the better for it.

Abraham Lincoln

To say that you behaved like animals is offensive to the animal creation because animals of the farmyard and field have an innate sense of decency.

Mr. Justice Cusack

Contents

Introduction

Introduction

Scapegoat is our carefully chosen word to shed our sins onto animals so only those deemed to be human always wins. Hence humans are born superior to ensure it is the human who is bound to win. The origin of the term is from the Day of Atonement which springs from a desire for reconciliation, to forget any differences between humans and thus to staunch the strife. In doing so the strife is settled with destroying an animal's life. For good measure it was much better to choose two goats. Then the first goat was spared by having the people's sins symbolically laid upon her as she was exiled into the wilderness. Then the second goat was nominated to be the one to be sacrificed. Each goat was chosen by a lot so their lot was to be faced with a future of exile or death. That was their lot as the losers whilst the lot of the winners was always favourable towards humans. Then and now and for our future, a constant atonement arose where we shift our sins onto those we choose who whilst we are born to win animals are always born to lose.

In the psychology of human interaction involving scapegoating a choice is made to inflict aggressively punitive abuse towards other vulnerable and weaker persons or groups. The crucial aspect of the behaviour is it is conducted towards others who are always in a position where they are vulnerable and ready-made victims. In that vein it can particularly apply to a child. Yet there is one essential difference: while a child might be hurt by an adult and become a scapegoat for his own faults, there are at least other adults and those in in authority who can and do come to their aid. Animals are not subject to that aid for the simple reason it is humans who cause and inflict and more importantly, gain from the scapegoating.

It is why *Born to Win* is confined to a defined advantage to us at the expense of all others:

> Unable as usual to see the tombstone graph
> Using a warped will we rush to write our epitaph
> The planet ghost revisits at an astronomical cost
> Frozen forever in a freedom locked in permafrost
> Seeking the whole we sold our soil for our soul
> A false solace prize we alone were born to win
> An idea of a life-long mission by killing our kin
> Our human oath set in stone only serves to prove
> Everyone and everything else were born to lose

Given that expiation of a sin is the reason for the practice, it shows at once that by law and philosophy and religion we fail all animals. We bend the language out of shape by wielding society's pliers to our advantage. Atonement in essence means sinners can be consistently pardoned. Whilst that is admirable and perhaps desirable by society's norms and function, it has to be appreciated in this context the human strength stems from an animal's inherent weakness. It is a perennial moral and legal power of the powerful over the powerless. So anyway you choose to look at it it is always resolved by the same principle: only humans have a legal role and status within our society. Only humans have a soul. Atonement and scapegoating are the twin sides of the same biased coin that we use as our currency of human cruelty and a counterfeit leitmotif for our animal abuse. Each arises because we deliberately fail to accept that animals are sentient beings who suffer too and in many ways are no different than humans. Our palate and profit is more important than principle as in law we finally prefer our strife to any animal's life. Scapegoat is closely linked to the term 'tragedy'. For tragedy is formed from two Greek words namely 'tragos' which relates to a goat and 'oide' as an ode which leads to a 'Goatsong'. In the dramatic plays of the Ancient Greeks the actors dressed in skins of goats to represent 'Satyrs', mythological deities with an excuse for hircine abuse. Both the Elder and Younger Dionysus were besotted with festivals and dramatic performances. Both were self-appointed tyrants who were equally notorious for their cultivated streak of cruelty. So a festival ended with an offering to themselves. As each had blood coursing through their veins that was colder than ice their vainglory was performed as each goat was sacrificed.

So we have at once the etymology of scapegoat which proves the inherent truth of their treatment buy us: Tragedy. It serves to remind the reader of *The Animals Film* Framed:

> The rebel poet's wound will never heal
> As *The Animal's Film i*s frozen forever
> On the broken-down spinning reel-to-reel
> The comedy is over let the tragedy begin

From then until now we effectively adopt the same aim and approach as is exemplified in the end on end verse of *Scapegoats towards Slaughter*:

When it comes to killing a stranger
If it is someone who is not your kind
Another species is seen as a money-changer
We use a Nelsonian eye to feign being blind

Bringing the goat's fate up to a later date can be seen in the foolish whimsical lies of Descartes, a vanity-stricken scientist cursed with a cold cold heart. Whilst he claimed *Cogito, ergo sum* ['I think, Therefore I am'], his philosophy was based on a lie. His claim that an animal's pain was non-existent and their screams, whilst being tortured by scientists like himself, was only as mechanical as a clock chime was wholly phoney. What is worst of all is that within his troubled heart the lie within his life was well-known to Descartes. He knew his philosophy was Janus-faced as he based his case on every animal he maligned as being a natural-born scapegoat. So for his followers he became the major source who validated the violence of vivisection. Although vivisection proves nothing except that all the exhibits experimented upon by descendants of Descartes are the 21st century Dionysian twisted beliefs in action. Descartes later confessed that his hypothesis was false. Even then it did not prevent him from experimenting on animals as an ancestor of Mengele. Animals were born to live and die as his eternal scapegoats.

On an allied parallel term which we now use exclusively for the Nazi's treatment of Jews, it is instructive to consider the etymology of the term introduced by historians in the1950's as 'the Holocaust'. The word holocaust is derived from the Greek holokauston from 'holos' and 'kaustos' meaning 'a burnt sacrifice offered to a god.' In Hellenistic religion they offered up animals who were burned alive as a sacrifice, offered by night and burnt in full. The reference drove Isaac Bashevis Singer to accurately assess that 'To animals we are all Nazi's and for them it is an eternal Treblinka.' As a tribute to him, the dictum is explored in *The 21st Century Treblinka*:

All we learn from those teachers
While living in our glitzy global Ritz
As their body shatters and mind splits
In our world as an Animals' Auschwitz

Our treatment of animals is steeped in and stems from the sophistry of the concept of the soul. All humans have a soul. No animal has a soul. While that is something which is neither proven to exist or be true, it is our reason for being biased towards humans and against animals. Notwithstanding that unassailable point it allows us to be part of a human conspiracy to assume a natural superiority over all animals. Our conspiracy of silence condemns those deemed by us to be soulless given it is mirrored in our self-serving morality and enshrined in legal speciesism.

Animals do not depend on us to exist. Animals should not depend upon us to survive except within the honesty of the law. Animals have their own reasons and seasons outside of ours. Might is never right when it is used purely to deny another body the legal right to live. All those factors and features play out in these shadow sketched epitaphs. Poetry serves as the historical Blakeian truth-teller that urges us to be the animals' voice. Even if justice is blind, we cannot conceal the truth for save to ease our collective coward conscience it never hurts the teller.

Who can dispute the inhumanity of hunting – of pursuing a poor defenceless creature for mere amusement, till it becomes exhausted by terror and fatigue, and of then causing it to be torn to pieces by a pack of dogs? From what kind of instruction can men, and even women, imbibe such principles as these? How is it possible they can justify it? And what can their pleasure in it consist of? Is it not solely in the agony they produce to the animal?...But what is the object of their pursuit? Is there any other than to torment and destroy?

Lewis Gompertz

Preface

Abridged from *Jungle Judge Justice* and *Blue-bird sings the Blues* and *An Animals' Charter*.

It is and always has been there lot to be exploited. They have been abused, burnt at the stake, hanged at the gallows, ill-treated, imprisoned, tried and executed as criminals, trained to kill, vivisected and used as weapons of war. They have been and are subjected to every kind of abuse imaginable for reasons of economics, hedonism, law, politics, religion, science, sport and war.

As to who and why the answer is the same. Animals are abused because they are animals.

English Law allows us to classify an animal as a 'thing'. Lacking a legal status renders an animal's voice as valueless as a ventriloquist's dummy. Animals are our artefacts because homo sapiens are actually homo sans sapience.

Vladimir Putin has decided that his decimation of Ukraine proves his character and provides a legacy of which he is proud. Putin has delusions he is a mix of Hitler and Stalin with a soupcon of Genghis Khan. In truth he is natural-born creepy character cursed with a gargantuan ego who is a political rag-and-bone-man. He is far from alone on the political stage as a sawn-off Pagliacci.

While following later research it is now more widely known, over 40 years ago a startling statistic exhibited a cruel characteristic of Russian criminals:

Out of 135 criminals, including robbers and rapists, 118 admitted that when they were children they burned, hanged, and stabbed domestic animals: *Voice of the Voiceless* [1979]

Putin has long seen Ukrainian people as his self-serving statistics of suffering. He has tried to prove his warped principles by a manufactured biased war in 2022. He sees them as Roman lawyers viewed slaves and animals. Roman lawyers defined a slave as someone who was in the *dominium* of another which meant they were merely property. The fact they were human was irrelevant to their ownership. Slavers who bought and sold slaves, assaulted and whipped and killed them, saw them as another 'thing' no different than a horse.

Susan Brownmiller in *Against Our Will* cites the true character of a Russian rapist. After he abducted and violated a woman he started to feel guilty and said, '*I am a big pig*'. He well knew he was not an animal at all. He was a typical cheap cynical creep as all rapists are and intent on finding an easy excuse for his abuse as all rapists do.

It is why we have a Metropolitan Police officer, Couzens, abduct and rape and murder a young defenceless woman. In truth Couzens treated her, as a judge condemned the action of another recent rapist, as 'a piece of meat'. Yet another serving Metropolitan Police officer, Cobban, replied to a fellow officer, 'I want to taser a cat and a dog to see which reacts better. Same with children. Zapp zap you little f***ers.'

An American study by *The Link* in 2022 enumerated the clear connection between animal abuse and violence towards people which have shown that:

100% of sexual homicide offenders examined had a history of cruelty towards animals.

70% of all animal abusers have committed at least one other criminal offense and almost 40% have committed violent crimes against people.

63.3% of men who had committed crimes of aggression admitted to cruelty to animals.

48% of rapists and 30% of child molesters reported committing animal abuse during childhood or adolescence.

Men who abused animals were five times more likely to have been arrested for violence towards humans, four times more likely to have committed property crimes and three times more likely to have records for drug and disorderly conduct offences.

Perpetrators of domestic violence often threaten to injure or kill pets as a way of controlling others in the family. The animal becomes a tool no different than being abused as an exhibit in a science lab or fodder in a factory farm, save for them being legal. In domestic violence cases the animal is abused to harass or silence the vulnerable person who cares for her pet. For the maximum suffering the perpetrator will hurt or kill her pet in her presence. A high proportion of battered women, from over 50% to over 70%, seeking shelter in a women's refuge state their partners hurt or killed a family pet. The violent man - rest assured it is usually a man - views a vulnerable and weak person as a reflection of a vulnerable and weak animal.

The same motive applies when an elderly relative and their pet is threatened or harmed. Equally it resonates with child abuse. There may be different objects the perpetrator wishes to achieve be it financial or sexual, but the end game method is the same namely to gain control and force a victim to comply with their threats in order to avoid their pet or themselves being assaulted.

According to *The Link* animal abusers will resort to hurting or killing animals to:

Prove their power and exercise control over the family;
Prevent the victim from leaving the family home or to return;
Degrade the victim by forcing them to abuse their own pet.

While there were no other human victims involved, it puts into perspective Kurt Zouma's assault on his pet Bengal cat by repeatedly hitting and kicking the fear-filled creature and shouting, *'I'll kill it. I swear I'll kill it.'* It is accentuated by getting his brother, Yoan, to film his violence and then arranging for the film to be on social media so it was broadcast to the world.

The Zouma brothers were obviously pleased and proud of their assault on his defenceless pet cat. The Zouma brothers added a dozen laughing emoji's. When Zouma's child held her he slapped the cat in and out of the child's hands. Neither of these characters, the Zouma brothers, seemed to have any understanding at all of the connection between racism and sexism and speciesism:

> While the victim's injuries still fester
> Indulging in a history of mass-misery
> The Zoumas betrayed their own ancestors

After the Zoumas uploaded their abuse of his pet cat, a spate of copycat crimes filled the social media. Their slavish imitators followed the Zoumas guide to being a football hero.

The view of a sharp shooter killer exemplifies the connection. A gunman went on a shooting rampage at the University of Montreal in 1980. He deliberately sought out female engineering students. He burst into a classroom shouting, 'You're women. You're going to be engineers. You're all a bunch of feminists. I hate feminists.' Then he killed a total of 14 women before turning the gun on himself. A woman who survived said, 'It was a human hunt. We were the quarry.' [*Animals and Cruelty and Law*: (1980)]

Pythagoras considered that killing an animal was 'murder'. Fifteen centuries later it remains true that animal abuse in childhood can certainly lead to murder.

Animals deserve respect because they are as Darwin found 150 years ago, 'The difference in mind between man and the higher animals, great as it is, certainly is one of degree and not of kind.' We prefer to practise the opposite of what we preach. As a result we deprive an animal of any legal status. We are experts in unethical martial arts who hold a black belt in dodging life and truth.

Apart from the A-Z of animal law and rights and welfare, from abattoirs to zoos, from butchers to crush movies, we are left with a crucial question which is best directed at the vivisectionist because what they do is legal. A pointed question encapsulates what we know and need to know about our abuse of animals:

Question: Why do you vivisect animals and torture them to death by your experiments on our behalf?
Answer: The data we gain is relevant and valuable to scientists because animals are like us.

Question: Why is it morally right for you to vivisect animals and torture them to death by your experiments on our behalf?
Answer: The data we gain is relevant and valuable to scientists and animals are not like us.

In the *Kiko Case* [2015] an American judge, Associate Judge Eugene Fahey, decided against a chimpanzee being entitled to 'personhood' [a 'legal personality' in English Law.] Later he reflected upon his decision and sought to justify it. Fahey attempted to share his 'dilemma' with his brother judges in the *Kiko Case*:

'Does an intelligent non-human animal who thinks and plans and appreciates life as human beings do have a right to the protection of the law against arbitrary cruelties and enforced detentions visited on him or her? This is not merely a definitional question, but a deep dilemma of ethics and policy that demands our attention.'

A seven-year-old child holding her new-born kitten could have told the judge that the animal was a living breathing creature and definitely not just a thing. Fahey's dilatory stance was pusillanimous. Why did he not have the courage of his judicial conviction at the time of his judgment?

Fahey's stance is dodo justice in action. It is the *Dred Scott Case* [1856] revisited where American judges declared slavery was moral and legal, save for two dissenting judges. A similar bold stance has now been taken in an Appeal *In The Matter of Nonhuman Rights Project v Brehen* [2022] where two American Judges, Rowan Wilson and Jenny Rivera, delivered their dissenting decisions in favour of an elephant, Happy, who should not be classed as a 'thing'.

Perhaps they have been listening to a seven-year-old child who holding her new-born kitten could have told any judge that an animal was a living breathing creature and definitely not just a thing. With time maybe the other judges will have ears that hear the cries of our modern-day slaves as their throats are slit in ritual slaughter or are exploded with a harpoon in scarlet scarred water. Any such child could have told any such judge anywhere in the world at any time that any such elephant, unless it is a cuddly stuffed Steiff, is not a thing.

Law is the only moral system that can save animals from their perennial enemies: us.

While the wraith of justice is fleeting it can be grasped by us making their legal slavery a matter of history. Poetry can be our skeleton key to open our eyes to our sad-eyed justice to see what we cannot see.

xxxxx

God is so wise that when she created birds she gave them complete freedom from the invisible chains of the sky. We are so wise that we prove our natural love of birds by confining them in cramped cages. Her spirit sailed through the swirling sea making it so wide that fish would be forever free. We value fish by catching them in the net of crime and time to place them in our holy prison of piracy and endless fiddle-de-dee.

Yet the lesson of dignity and respect due to the reason animals inhabit the world is all around us. They were here long before us and will remain when our epitaphs are hidden by wind-blown unkempt sprawling weeds.

One who knew that unassailable truth is a French woman who, when she heard the word, sided with and chided her husband to rescue an injured bird. Stephane Mahe witnessed how Xavier Bouget was accompanied by Blanchon, a white female pigeon, as he tended to his daily duties including nibbling on a hobnob, watering his garden and tinkering in his workshop. She was even by his side when he cycled in the countryside. Blanchon is always there. She was befriended by Bouget when she was a frightened chick. Now she has become his constant companion. She perches parrot-style on his shoulder as well as walking with him. They met when Bouget saw her trying to escape from a cat. He went home and told his wife what he saw. She chided him on why he had not rescued the bird. So he went back, did so and took Blanchon home in his pocket. Everyone now asks him how he trained the bird to be so tame. He explains 'there is no trick just mutual respect'. He claims anyone can do the same if 'they respect the animal for what it is, that is a living creature that shares the Earth with us.'

Bouget said, 'You just need to be patient, to understand how they live and adapt to their life, because they will adapt to yours.' We have a lot to learn from him as he willingly shared the wisdom of his grand age, having lived for eight decades.

Birds have always been abused by us. The creeps who trap birds with a lime to use them as decoys to trap bigger birds show the callous core of our vulture society dressed up in an attempt to pass it off as culture. The 'Birdman of Alcatraz' was acclaimed for his rehabilitative venture as a self-taught ornithologist. Yet he was incarcerated because he had committed a crime, namely murder. What crime had the birds used in his 'research' committed except for their nature's fortune in being born?

It resonates with the vicars gathering at Christmas where the various birds disappear as swiftly as if they had voluntarily flown down the diners' throats. The birds are devoured as if they were a glorious gift from God as some self-ordained sacred sacrifice.

Where animals are concerned, women who are professed feminists often have not learned the reason for feminism.

It is magnified in sharp focus by the self-proclaimed feminist Caitlin Moran who boasted in 2015 about her feelings towards her 'rescued' cat, Betty: 'I am a cat hater. I hate my cat...God, I hate that cat.' She devoted her complete column to the same theme. Later in 2019 she referred to how she had been told by her father to kill a fish. As a child she accompanied him on a fishing trip until the day 'a gudgeon swallowed the hook too enthusiastically making it impossible to get out'. He told her to kill the fish. He 'barked' at her: 'Do it! It's in *agony. Finish it off*!' She tried to 'stove its head in' with a rubber torch. Following that childhood 'traumatic experience' she quit fishing. Until 2019 when as a mature adult she was 'eager to show off my skills' yet again.

Alice Walker says all that a genuine feminist needs to know to be true to their self: 'The animals of the world exist for their own reasons. They were not made for humans any more than black people were made for whites or women for men.'

Politicians' ephemeral promises prove animals are legal canaries in our social mines. It is why her timeless tune is proof the blue-bird was born to sing. All it takes is a single shot from someone with a sawn-off soul who blasts her from the blood-spilled skies. It is not hard to figure that regardless of who is the one that holds the gun, we use our shared vision and vigour to pull the trigger.

xxxxx

Bo Diddley sang with his mesmeric rasping blues plea for understanding by his lover claiming, 'You can't judge a book by the Cover'. While no one would wish to doubt the evergreen Diddley, that is untrue here as species of the grebe portrayed were hunted to death by vainglorious women seeking fine feathers for their snook-cocked hats.

We condemn other species for no reason except that is what they are by birth. Human rights are beyond price because with them people can live and die freely with dignity. Equally without them people are fettered by the chains of law and subjugation. Animal rights share the same purpose within a human prison for the same reason.

Racism is evil because it devalues and prejudges people without a valid cause. Sexism is base as it discriminates against humans purely as a matter of biology. Speciesism originates from a similar source as racism and sexism. Yet it is worse as a form of prejudice because animals need us to resist our prejudice in order to live their lives. Animals are denied legal rights because they are hamstrung by being denied a human tongue.

The connection between racism and sexism and speciesism is they are bound together by our bond of bias. The arguments we base on race and sex, including biological differences and inferiority and intelligence, are equally applicable to animals. Why then do most human victims of personal prejudice fail to identify with their animal counterparts? You may well ask why self-proclaimed feminists feel it is fine to shaft animals by eating and wearing them? Is that the spirit of Wollstonecraft? You might ask why religious zealots practise their beliefs by sacrificing animals? Is it simply that we can use and abuse those unable to climb the first rung of our legal ladder?

Animals are our victims before birth and only cease being so after their death. For our actions against animals are prejudicially sutured within the sinews of our society. Law as the only social instrument that could protect their rights denies them a role and status. Instead we dilute and limit their power by claiming to promote their 'welfare'. We prefer welfare to granting animals 'rights' as it allows us to continue using our conspiratorial strength over their vulnerability and weakness.

Over two hundred years ago the poet Soame Jenyns identified the butcher as a reflection of his work and our lack of feeling: 'The butcher knocks down the stately ox with no more compassion than the blacksmith hammers a horse-shoe, and plunges his knife into the throat of an innocent lamb with as little reluctance as the tailor sticks his needle into the collar of a coat.' Then as now legally the horse is no different than the steel shoe that shod her feet or indeed the knife that took her life.

That is why in 2024 we still legally classify an animal in the time-immemorial phrase as a '*thing*'. That they bleed and breathe is conveniently forgotten if that fact clashes with our preternatural greed and need for profit. We ignore the fact they have a heartbeat and a pulse for the same reason. Our view is shaped and shared by a natural conspiracy where all humans take advantage of all animals for no other reason than just because we can.

That focus is sharpened when you consider the lame pathetic television programmes for general consumption where the contestants had to breed and kill their own animals. Why? There is no reason except that it appeals to the viewer plus who among the victims can object to their fate? These crass 'reality' shows use the colloquial 'creepy crawlies' to scare contestants and amuse easily-pleased voyeuristic viewers. It is a small step away from the black and white minstrel shows and wife-selling auctions. Taking advantage of those creatures that are within our control is always a form of bullying. In 2020 we had 'Meat the Family' which is the same concept with the same format for the same reason. It would be unacceptable if it was now practised on a non-consenting human. No objection could be made by any of the actual victims as by then the animals were just more statistics of misery as the main meal.

As it involves the 'family' rather than an anonymous animal abuser, the viewer has the advantage of seeing their collective palate as the yardstick by which they jointly decide to kill and eat their 'pet'. The lesson that animals have no value beyond being human food is underlined by the mother preparing and sharing the bodies of those pets. The echoing laughter around the table verifies the value of the social occasion. Children as viewers and better still as part of the family, immediately learn the life lesson that animals have no value as living creatures. Their value is gauged by a body on the plate.

In 2020 a Chinese entertainment company threw a pig to the ground in a bungee jump. The Chinese crowd 'laughed and jeered' while the falling pig was 'squealing in terror'. The company claimed it was 'just fun, entertainment'. If it is such 'fun' why are their employees not trussed up with their feet bound and then forced off exactly as the pig was by them? The 'fun' finished when the pig was duly slaughtered.

Niklas Ekstedt, a chef, extolled the virtues of eating live creatures: 'It freaks out my British friends when we toast bread over a flame, slather it in honey and then lay it on an ants nest. You wait for the ants to crawl over the toasts stick – especially the acidic fat red ones – and then eat them while they are writhing and wriggling! Delicious!' No doubt even Ekstedt roasted and toasted over a barbecue cauldron would have a certain appeal for a passing discerning cannibal.

Similarly Hirst placed a formaldehyde animal in a tank and live butterflies in a locked room with no means of escape to prove his natural artistry. The title of his Exhibition, 'In and Out of Love', proves he fails to understand the import of words. During one experiment Hirst sacrificed 900 butterflies. All of it proves it is problematic to distinguish any gifted latter-day Rembrandt from a self-serving practitioner of art with a capital 'F'.

Legally the animals' lives and future count for nothing. They are not even social pawns in a political game. Animals are less than pawns because they are not part of our plan which is comprised of rules made by and for us. We decide who can share the benefit and who will bear the burden. We dictate the state of society's game plan so animals are bound by our ball and their chain.

A dung beetle is as important and unimportant to the planet as a human. When the last human is dead the fimetic world will still exist. When the last dung beetle is dead, will the world disappear? We figure we are at the top of nature's ladder, when we are just part of the universe with most species being more vital to the continuation of the world than us. Thors Hanson went travelling with his son, Noah, on a journey to discover bees and ecology. Noah made an observation that so struck Hanson he had nothing to add. He made it the last sentence of his book, *The Buzz* [2018]: 'The world can live without us, but we can't live without bees.'

In the *Hull Prison Riot Case* [1979] counsel for the defendant submitted that society was to be judged by how it treated its lowest members. The Court of Appeal agreed. Lord Justice Shaw said that although they were prisoners they still had rights as 'The courts are in general the ultimate custodians for the rights and liberties of the subject whatever his status and however attenuated those rights and liberties may be as a result of some punitive or other process.' The principle is right. However, the judgment is wrong. Animals are the lowest members of our society. How a society treats its weakest members reflects its strength. Are the weak to perish or be protected by the strong? It is a question to be resolved by compassion and compromise and conscience.

Law is our leveller in the pursuit of justice. The worst crime a human being can commit against another human being is murder as it deprives the victim of the right to live. In the 16th century Leonardo said, 'I have from an early age abjured the use of meat, and the time will come when men such as I will look upon the murder of animals as they now look upon the murder of men.' Precisely the same arguments used against granting animals legal rights were used against the abolition of slavery by the slave traders. Who would now argue for slavery? For if you would then you equally have to be prepared for someone else to believe it would be a good idea to make you a slave. Human rights and animal rights are closely linked as two sides of the same coin of compassion.

Any question we ask and answer we give about animals within our society and our abuse of them has to be predicated on the basis of Darwin's classic statement in the *Descent of Man*: 'There is no fundamental difference between man and the higher mammals in their mental faculties...The lower animals, like man, manifestly feel pleasure and pain, happiness and misery....'

In *Swan* Mary Oliver asks the body-blow clincher question we must all ask ourselves: 'And have you too finally figured out what beauty is for? And have you changed your life?' Yet where animals are concerned we have still not learned that in the seeds of their destruction we sow our own.

Welfare as a concept is of little value to animals. Welfare might allow them to have a bigger cage or more links in a chain, but they are still subject to our terms during their lives. Rights are the only answer for all animals as a guarantee they can live and die with dignity. We have forged a relationship with animals as we had with slaves. Given the choice we chose to be parasitic rather than symbiotic. One moment we are willing to vivify them, next moment we are willing to kill them. We are content to ignore the impure truth that one woman's meat is another animal's death.

Whether they are a Great Dane or an Irish wolfhound, be they domestic or wild, on a farm or on a plate, in a laboratory or in us, animals touch our daily lives in every sense. As that includes the economic and political and social sense, it is bound to be reflected in the legal one too. Animals are inextricably connected with us, so naturally we use our power to control them by law. We use a false logic in all of our treatment of animals. Hence we defend the indefensible and justify the unjustifiable by a conspiracy that all humans share to a greater or lesser degree. We openly take advantage of two related limbs namely animals are vulnerable because they have no legal voice and we deprive them of having a legal voice. We conspire against animals possessing a legal voice by our silence. Our conspiracy is borne because we all gain from their birth. Our ability to take advantage of animals allows us to practise abuse as our legal *mores*.

English colonials figured it was acceptable in 1619 to 'buy' 20 Angolans who had been kidnapped by the Portuguese. The enslaved Africans that were bought in the British colony of Virginia on 20 August marked the start of slavery in the New World that lasted for 250 years – or more accurately, for 400 years. Our ancestors acted in that manner for these related reasons: they saw the black slaves as a trading commodity no different than animals; they could get away with it because the black slaves had no legal voice; the conspiracy of the traders usurped any compassion for the human cargo.

In 2024 the same principle is followed by those who avoid finding a fashion that fails to bleed. Even those who oppose animal abuse and would never condone cruelty to them in any form would in the next breath reach for a hamburger or parade peacockish in a fur coat stolen from the first owner while she was still wearing it to stay alive. It is a zwischenzug move we make with a blindfold to prove we intentionally fail to taste the truth.

A Black Cat Photograph

They do not photograph well at all
When you want to boast
A black cat is just toast
It blends in with the background
So it just becomes a dark rebound
And affects your profile on the social
So you seem to be a bit parochial
And who wants any chit-chat
From a troll for choosing a black cat
Better to go for one who is an aristocrat

You want a thing that looks good
In the photograph as it should
So give the sad black cat a miss
Turn away and never turn back
Because no creature ever looks good
In a photo or a shoot if it is black
You better turn off and turn your back
It is better with one that is white
You can even see them at night
And no one gets bad luck or a fright

While a cat you have to feed each day
It is not worth it what you have to pay
Because they become a messy mound
Whether at the back or in the foreground
On several levels you are much better off
Walking on and leaving the litter behind
Tomorrow you could get a ginger one with a bell
Or maybe a tabby or even a striped tortoiseshell
It is so much easier to clothe them for fun

Yes you can dress them up for a belly-laugh
The bonus is they make a great photograph

It is a bit like an ageing seaside beauty queen
No one wants to choose an acne-ridden teen

Though we do not kill the contestants
We could choose that course for cats
Not unlike most animal sanctuaries do
When we say 'not today'
To any cat that is black
Then walk away and never look back
The sanctuary and cat can take the fall
Remember it is only an animal after all

If people were selected
So those too ugly to live
Were instantly rejected
Who among the rabble
Would ever be elected
Who would a hungry hobo
Or a blind beggar choose
Among our batch of politicos
If she wanted desperate alms
To cross her upturned palm
Might she then perhaps even prefer
A jet black cat in a cellar at midnight
Straight as a razor with her honest purr

If everyone rejects the black cat
In no time the sanctuary will fall
Then we will have a better choice
When the black cats all go to the wall

Their lives are mapped out in our graph
We need a cat for a laugh in a photograph

Even a black cat is okay in its own way
Much as a stuffed panda or teddy bear
But when it gets old and scraggy
With mangy fur and a body that is baggy
Much as with some old coffin-dodger
Whose use is passed as he has had his day
Passed their sell-by date as a lifetime-lodger
You can hand him back because he is black
He could find bliss in a hospice
As any cat that has had their day
Or if that is too much trouble
Add it to the rubble and slowly walk away

A Canterbury Story

Chaucer told a worthy tale
Of a cock and a certain ruse
That Hemingway would often use
An ego that only praise would sate
And an appetite for animal abuse
That could not wait
As he found the flood
Of someone else's blood
Would make his heart beat
Just a little faster
And so it is no disaster
And equally as a blaster
It is no surprise his own demise
Came from a ritual borne
Of the scorching mid-day sun
But ratcheted up to at least a ton
He hoped the killing of a bull
Would not be limited to one

With that optimistic thought
He had no time for a wreathe
When he brushed his teeth
With a sawn-off shotgun

His faithful dog pawed at the bathroom door
Until the hinges could not hold it any more
Broke in and waited by his master on the floor
Yet love is not the way of Hemingway
Who only found personal glory
In his bitter souped-up story
Of killing for killings sake

But listen and perhaps learn
A lesson of what is true
Perhaps in his own way
Hemingway is no different
Than me and you

A Catechism Creed

John Smith was just a child
When his father taught him
How to shoot deer in the wild
Killing both of them with vim

When he shot a bird of paradise
As she fell he felt pure guilt
A flood of tears filled his eyes
His conscience bit him to the hilt

John Smith went into the box
To make his first confession
Said his conscience still rocks
The priest then ruined the session

He said concern for a bird
You have no reason for guilt
Caring for a pox is so absurd
When birds are only flying silt

John Smith knew that his religion
Had no place in his wounded heart
Without care for a wounded pigeon
His start backed the horse not the cart

The priest in that first confession
Taught him a lasting life lesson
One that he would never forget
He learned the cost of compassion

When no one counts in any amount
Life has its own price for each debt
Yet it remains one that has to be repaid
Yes it remains a debt that must be met

All animals are our heaven's gift
We do not have to steal or lift
We do not have to sort or sift
Seeing his eyes skyward shift
The child saw the priest's drift

Selling his story as a narcotic for many
Given free as the people's natural dope
The priest paraded a prayer for a penny
Granted by each pope as new old rope

Sold with the chalice from a gilded palace
Selling a blessed sight of food as their hope
Just another well-timed evangelistic trope
As vital as a vision in a broken periscope

A Claim to a Name

It may well be that
Man gave names to all the animals
Whether they were in a cage
Or the jungle or a kennel
And whether they turned out
To be a cat or a camel
And named after a cigarette
Or the choppy Channel
But those points flow a bit close to the master
Taking advantage of a natural human disaster
Of the Massa to rename a slave
The captives of war or our trade
For whom the price was paid
In the links of a clanking chain
On being the vanquished
Then feeling the victor's rain
To stay in their lane
That is a continuing wrong
Whatever the raid or a fight
Given a namc to make it right
Changes nothing for someone
On the outside who will never belong

So the right to call
Any other creature by a name
Is a claim that fixes and forms and tames
By those who forge the game and frame
When morality falls to slumber
The gain of that hidden rain
Outweighs the captive's pain

As each creature becomes a number
Marginal forever as a forever criminal
The ID photo by us as nature's police
Make them the victims of our caprice
Devoid of choice and voice
A slave with an unpaid invoice
The Massa with his whip
Lash-on-lash on each hip
Held in check with a halter
So their freedom never falters
As we fleece goose-grease and geese
We are their forever Massa
Incarnate slavers as their mouthpiece

A Colston con meets a sapient Swan

The people saw his deeds in neo-neon
Colston was a symbol of slavery as an icon
A twin combination of a monster and a moron
His grave should be visited by everyone
Who know his trader's routes and roots
Then danced upon wearing hobnail boots

A man whose ethos sailed through his crooked colon
Whose statue was hissed by a Bristol harbour swan
Glad his statue sunk quicker than a boulder
A graffiti painted hollow figure served as a trigger
For her to sit on his sagging shrugged shoulder

For a hate that was washed by scum and soon gone
The murky dock swamp showed his life as a total con
A medal pinned to his chest he could not hide
His tombstone truth serves to prove
There is no pride in genocide
No wonder the swan used his surly face to sit upon
While taking time out to wash and to preen
She noticed his thin-lipped mouth looked obscene
So she shook her feathers like a fiery tambourine
Then used his traitor's face as a ready-made latrine

A Creed of Claudette Colvin

Fired by her baptism
She was caught between
Fighting the face of racism
Or a climb-down surrender
That could bend and break her
On a cold day in March 1955
Her spirit truly came alive
She would not take a dive
Claudette Colvin at just 15
She was born with a rebel mind
She was no white man's slave
She was no black man's pet
She was 100% her own girl
The world would find out yet

Sitting with three friends on the bus
The white driver told them to move
Without causing any kind of fuss
Move to the back as is your place
Any black face in the white space
Struck a cuss in the driver's craw
To see any black and any squaw
All in all it was an instant williwaw
Claudette knew it was against the law

Claudette was caught in a legal trap
Her mind was a mixed-up moral map
Saying 'sorry' and then forced to move
What could or would it serve or prove
She might move an Uncle Tom in town
Or should she stay standing up

11

Fighting for her rights by sitting down
A time when her life ran out of rhyme
Colvin was no puppet or clown
Colvin's concern did not linger
Staring at the driver's pointed finger
She was ready to sing her own song
She knew in her heart what was right
She knew in her soul he was wrong
Her friend A moved to the back
Her friend B feared arrest too
Holding their heads low slunk away
C feared arrest too if she stayed
She did not intend to offend
So she too scurried to the back
Where the seats were reserved
For people deemed to be inferior
Unlike whites born to be superior
Unlike blacks as a passing plasma
For people deemed black anathema
All in all no different than animals
Her friends sat behind the white folks
While her irc was poked and stoked

Claudette sat on the bus in the front
In downtown Montgomery Alabama
The lesson learned at her mother's knee
Circled her mind knowing she was free
Told by her Mama every day in every way
'Listen, you may be born with black skin
But Honey you're as good as all of them
No better, but you sure ain't no worse
Let me tell you being black ain't a curse'

Colvin steeled herself and sat tight
As always she was ready for a fight
Knowing her old Mama was right
She stared dead-eyed at the driver
Her flint face reflecting life's race
Straight into his white glinting face
She stayed sitting tight in her space
She said so others heard her case
'I paid for a seat I ain't going to go
To the back where blacks are on show
You'd better know I am not your negro'

Claudette knew if she moved to the back
It would be an act she would forever regret
Claudette was no white or black man's pet

On one shoulder she had Harriet Tubman
On the other she had Sojourner Truth
On the thundering Underground Railroad
She saw each ghost of justice as an omen
Claiming to the world 'Ain't I a Woman'

Colvin stayed in her seat
Colvin planted her feet
Until without seeking favour or fuss
She was dragged right off the bus
Two burly cops and almost concussed
Handcuffed and taken to the jailhouse
Locked in a cell so the past criminals
Left her overcome by the stale smell
Deprived even of a mattress and sleep
Her head started to swim and swell
She thought about 'heaven and hell'

To teach her a lesson to remember
She was denied a blanket and food
She was a target for pointed insults
Crass and crude and racist and rude
Practised insults blunt and sharp
Revolved inside her head
Lewd and intended to intrude
Yet for her their words did not count
Their swaggering mood and attitude
Sweaty jailers with nothing to prove
Locked inside their own false pride
Born of a congenital societal groove
All her companions moved giddy-up
Now was not the time to fit or quit
She stayed sitting as the face of injustice
Supped her freedom from a broken cup

Thrown off and under their bus
A stance that made her dance
Yet for her it was ever thus
So every black voice could sing
Flying with Colvin's freedom wing

The driver saw her as one
Only fit to sit at the back
Or on the stained floor
So the smell of a cell
Was similar to an abattoir
They sought to destroy her mind
Yet Claudette had such insight
She saw truth and law were blind
She knew she was not a criminal
She knew if you were born black

It was an everyday gimcrack
Or worse were born an animal
Stalked as if you were a humpback
Open prejudice was never subliminal
When you were caught in the trammel

The cops and jailers failed in the end
Well-deserved in the way life wends
In 2021 Colvin's conviction was quashed
Her stance on injustice now runs free
It is time to rejoice in her choice
Declared innocent at the age of 88
Her voice reverberates in world history
Her voice unlocked what it is to be free
When the good and bad flashes
When the right and wrong clashes
Each one has to decide
Which side you are on
Whether you are weak or strong
Are you one more silent coward
Yellow-belly colour of custard
Or will you sing with force
Until you are almost hoarse
A rebel yell to match the boys of Wexford
Singing loud and long your voice as strong
As the rebellion in Claudette Colvin's song
Taught Rosa Parks to take a rebel stance
Taught Martin Luther King to hold a lance
Taught the redneck racists her rebel dance
Taught the Klan that they had no chance
An echo of her stance as a life-long hellion
Resisting the chains of anyone's dominion
Her spirit in a 21st century animal rebellion

Her chimes of freedom are forever rung
For those born to die in agony too young
Sing for those who are forever hamstrung
By being born without a human tongue

A Crush on the Movies

To call her sick is far from enough
To call her evil is not rough enough
To call her obtuse does not begin to grapple
The sour apples hanging in her empty chapel
Whose sermon only delivered its hate
Untimely and as usual a laced bait

She smiled while the kitten took its last breath
As her high heels crushed the kitten to death
Then she put her hipster clothes back on
Collected her money saying 'see you honey'
To the pervert making the film in colour
To match the model and make it fuller

When the machine screeched into the night
Making copy-on-copy that would soon take flight
Among the perverts and paedophiles whose smiles
At the killing of a kitten crushed in a sleaze push
Would provide a rush until the next killing slush
Would satisfy their soiled spoiled porno wiles

Aided and abetted by a woman too crass to realise
She was Jim Crow revisited whatever was her pay
She was a rainbow shadow of the modern KKK
Has she forgotten the Tulsa Massacre in 1921
A century later the same gun was used in 2021
Has she forgotten the body of Adam Toledo
Killed by a cop as just one more 'so-so'
Has she forgotten the body of Daute Wright
Cut down in his prime in broad daylight
Has she seen a reflection of her own deception

Where in the scales of what is black and white
No in-between pose if truth is forced out of sight
One act is always wrong and one is always right

She fondles the wad of cold used cash
The price of a life she stole
Counting each note of the whole
What she has won and lost on the lash
The mathematics of her misery
Is plain for all to see
Her gain in filling a sadist's role
She counts the cost to her sold-out soul

Just like *The Zong* of her drowned ancestors
Just like the history of her past still festers
Just like Martha White saw black was right
Just like the peddler who is vice-bitten
Just like her pornographic heart is written
Just like her being rose-tinted dollar-smitten
Just like failing to be a frontline protester
Just like being another Massa molester
Just like stiletto heels in her coloured skcleton
Just like killing a defenceless piebald kitten
She has crushed the skin of her history
She has pushed the Jim Crow memory

A Deadhead Prize for Losers

Target animals denied any escape
As fish in a barrel seeing a bullet
A double-barrelled blast at a pullet
A ready-made target of holiday rape
Lurking on the hunters' landscape
Elephants are always in the room
As blatant as a mass-bigamist
Masquerading as an honest groom
In a bullet-riddled elephant tomb
As a culture creed of defined cruelty
They shoot and we by silence agree

Robin Hurt at the age of 76
Found a way to get his kicks
Boasts about how much it pays
Selling Britons an annual holiday
A safari where lives are there to take
Where all you meet are genuinely fake
Touring Africa to kill other creatures
Death is a core of the brochure features
A Londoner with a sound eye for profit
Makes sure Brits cannot miss a trophy
Big and close and defenceless to hit
How little wisdom he has learned
At the over-ripe bingo age of 76
Drips kinship blood in killing for kicks

Dickie Mac smiles and boasts about
The targets killed on his walkabout
A trophy denied to the timid cissies
Pride in his 700 trophies of 29 species

19

He has handily arranged to be killed
With a philosophy too readily billed
'Hunters are the best conservationists'
Which is akin to saying that scientists
Because they are degree-laden butchers
Actually conserve and preserve animals
Being butchers as well as vivisectionists
Or Putin is a model Pulitzer Prize pacifist

Abuse they dress up as 'conservation'
Language strangled beyond any meaning
Mountains of money they all crave
Pyramids of animals in a mass grave
Palmer and Vorster are bred the same
Ugly hearts without a heart to shame
Who crow about a vast bank account
Based on the head of a dead lion
Their main pride is a mane to mount
Their collective epitaph is plain
Each one hurt by nature and pain
They know they hold a trophy for losers
Of the lives they have wasted as abusers
Under a bare bulb light after a one-eyed fight

In a harsh honest 3 a.m. heat of a long night
Rest assured there is never an escape
No defence to a mass nature wild rape
A thirst for killing that remains parched
Until our politicians sate all the oligarchs
Moscow tombstones littered by bullying bruisers
We support Putin's boast 'I am an animal abuser'
Every heart-struck mirror is their refuser
Alone they fall together as their own accuser

A Dog is just for Christmas

A Dog is just for Christmas
He'll amuse you with each caper
Then at the end of the day
Just chuck him away with the ripped wrapping paper

A Dog is just for Christmas
A living present for the day
Then when you're bored by her bark
Park in the dark and dump her on a motorway

A Dog is just for Christmas
A gift with a sense of sorrow
You can play with it all day
And decide to just toss it aside tomorrow

A Dog is just for Christmas
Much like the tinsel and the tree
Then when the day is over
You can just dump him with the rest of the debris

A Dog is just for Christmas
A rescued pooch the perfect pet
A gift you don't have to lift
Yet can sling him out without a trace of regret

A Dog is just for Christmas
Put another log on the fire
We'll have ashes to ashes
When you put another dog on the funeral pyre

A Dog is just for Christmas
Too good a taste to waste it's true
Stuff a mutt in the oven
To celebrate the Feast the way the Chinese do

A Dog is just for Christmas
A truth that's as pure as litmus
Roast the mutt with the turkey
Then we'll have the cutest quirky Chinese Christmas

A Dog is just for the Pandemic

A Dog is just for the Pandemic
He lied to those at the sanctuary
Then he needed some company
Now the day came to cast aside the stray
Tied to a lamppost then casually walked away

A Dog is just for the Pandemic
It's so cute on the sparky Instagram
You can meet and greet in a flim-flam
Then when he had to go back to work
Sent her to a sanctuary as a knee-jerk scam

A Dog is just for the Pandemic
When you feel lonely and have no job
A dog does not care if you are a slob
But when he worked out what she had cost
Took her to the Motorway where she was lost

A Dog is just for the Pandemic
You can take him for a walk everyday
They will be loyal and listen to what you say
But the beauty is when their race has been ran
You can just get rid of it just because you can

A Dog is just for the Pandemic
They are great for playing in the park
And you feel safe with them in the dark
But when they scratch the furniture and trunk
You have to sling them out as so much junk

A Dog is just for the Pandemic
It is nonsense to say you have it for life
After all it is just a pooch not a wife
And when you have a new baby and all
A mutt is a burden if she's learning to crawl

The question is no longer academic
An animal is just part of the epidemic
It is not worth any moral polemic
After the success of the vivisection vaccination
Put the pooch in a pool on a permanent vacation

A Dog is just for the Pandemic
The solution is plain and systemic
Forget any sentiment if it is 'dangerous'
They are already far too numerous
And when you are out on a Sunday jolly
Let it off a leash and spend your lolly
If it happens to bite someone
At least you can get rid of her
In some grumpy judge's court
Where she will get a legal penance
When the thing will be sentenced
It is only the death of a pet for your folly
Who cares as next time you can be choosy
You could even click and collect a collie

A Dry Dog in a Wet Market

Scavenging on the street for something to eat
Anything whether it was sour or sweet
Hoping to escape from the people's wrongs
When caught by a gloved human tong
Then strung up in a crowded cage
Saw her as part of their weekly wage
One by one turned each life's stage
Dog after dog taken without a care
Until she was the last one huddled there
When they tried to grab her she resisted
The more they used force with a cruel twist
Catching her hard with the jagged tongs
So her pangs were sharp and prolonged
A matter they held without a heavy heart
For the more the pain the more the gain
The higher the heat the sweeter the meat
So the stray struggled as they juggled
With her will as the prize in their eyes
Which she wanted to do all she could
To stay inside the stained cramped cage
As her last ditch wish to deprive
Them of their wish to thrive
On one more dry dog to disbud
Drenched in her own spurting blood
In the wet scarlet market place
Served to dribble down their face
For if they ever got her outside
She would become someone's insides
She knew as sure as eggs is eggs
She would have no chance to survive
Against their intent to skin her alive

A Fish Out Of Water

'Fishing is my way of breathing' said Ted Hughes
Casting a line and a lie savouring his views
The poetry of prejudice as his fuse
It is a shame fish do not feel the same
While Hughes may breathe easier with his muse
Using poetry as a talent to abuse
The fish has no one to mourn in the pews
Hughes claimed fish were cold
Putting his conscience on hold
A tale at odds with one Plath told
Checking the corpse he had caught
His crooked hook making her life nought
Hughes gloried in his deathly news
Finding fun in how fish fought to live
Giving him a reason and rhyme for his ruse
A crowd gathered round his bloodied body
A macabre greed greater than any need
A lost lonely fish with nothing left to lose
Easing Hughes troubled heart with speed
Finding solace when a victim pays his dues
When Hughes breathed his last he could use
A certain truth whilst his losing body stews
His breath stops a fish from living
It is a carp he cannot hide
Hughes past proves his breathing
Is a way of life while his victim died
Fishing and wishing as a catch perishes
A slaughter in water of his scum tide
All he seems to have gained from pain
A self-serving pathetic phoney pride
Breathing hubris poetry no boast can hide

A Gift Horse

See the bright blood in the snow
Mixes so well with the flow
Now the fire's caught fast by the flood
There's much too much snow in her blood

Red clouds of dust fill the phial
Her face saves no trace of a smile
Her purple lips suck one more breath
Her vein's kissed by our Iscariot of death

Pull the lever that sends the shock
Make it max while they are in hock
We have to conceal our addiction
An electric cure for our infliction
Line up all the caged exhibits
So we can be as ever chrematistic
As well as academic and voyeuristic
Yet equally become more egotistic
Collect the data from our statistics
A prize for our science community
Our glee revealed by their ecstasy
One million repeated experiments
To add to the millions already spent
As head and heart is twisted and bent
Each head and heart is a broken token
Mixed-up in a torrent of our torment

The torture is rough and gets rougher
Anything as long as we do not suffer
Smoke plumes drift and hit the sky
The carcass of one who had to die

A blade cuts a line on the mirror
Each sliced for our junkie whim
A bargain as each scientist finds
Another exhibit as one more victim
True value as an animal pays the price
A bargain as we win and they lose their skin
We get the presents as they pay the penance
For us an absence counts for so much less
Than our scalpel demand for their presence
The expert leads the exhibit to their death
Each expert borrows morals from Macbeth

Let's inject the poison in our veins
Let's addle our brains with cocaine
Then we can vivisect caged animals
Then we can free all our criminals
Claim it is an illness not a crime
A useless lie to protect our paradigm
Our pain in them is no contradiction
For our predilection of our addiction

As we inject more and more snow
A needle and a rush of the red flow
Send millions of innocent creatures
As our favourite science features
Their blood being spilt for our guilt
An excuse in our false solace of skunk
Dead-head conscience as our legal junk
Then no one who counts can ever flunk
Using a premeditated animals mega-death
Our daily doped doppelganger ersatz death

See the bright blood in the snow
Mixes so well with the flow
Now the fire's caught fast by the flood
There's much too much snow in her blood

A Green River Killer Revisited

The advance of a rudderless ship
With no one competent at the tiller
Every child can become the President
Yet misreading the legal crumbling pillar
Leads to a crass view of their Constitution
So every creep can become a serial killer
By misinterpreting the 'right to bear arms'
As a perverse solecistic legal prostitution

Yet rest assured as with our American cousins
England breeds creeps by the sixes and dozens
Ian Brady had a heart of grimy granite
When it came to killing he would pan it
To sift a victim according to his whim
His favourite was climbing to a top flat
Then find another trusting purring cat
Then fling the creature through the air
Laughing as like the last one she went splat
Sprawled dead in blood on a 'Welcome' mat
Until he found someone better than that
A friendly trusting child as a substitute cat
When Brady started his plan to torture children
He had the benefit of the warped Myra Hindley
She matched and surpassed his penchant for killing
Starting with poison and strangling hungry pigeons
Waiting for the one who was eager to feed them
They soon found out her fondness to seed them
When they died before her eyes she just juggled
A love for their pain she indulged in again and again
Together Brady and Hindley became a killing duo
A hatred of children burned bright day and night

Catching the disease of conceit to feed their might
No difference between an animal and a child
All that mattered was their victims
Were vulnerable and could be defiled
What really set them alight
So each could sew and grow
Their rancid seed of killing children
Made each other's savage heart thrive
Half-satisfied when few were left alive
Feeding their intent as a killers' bent

From Bundy to Dahmer and Ridgway to Spencer
Each used a different method yet no less tenser
All had the same aim to find someone alone
Offer a lift or a gift or a bed in their home
Where between being an animal
Or a passing defenceless stranger
Was the same to each criminal
Presenting an ever pressing danger
Each in their own way just another clone
A life route and death chosen as an offshoot
Their rotten fruit was just the same
When it came to burying the bones
Finding someone weak and random to kill
An animal or a child was grist to their mill

When the scales are balanced with weight
The sordid saga of killers heavy with hate
Torturing children and animals
As fully-fledged inbred criminals
Death-smells filter through fear and sheer terror
When any life ends by a knife or in an abattoir

A fact that hits with an immediate impact
Without an excuse or escape from the truth

Huntley was the same as the rest
His aim to use strength to wrest
The lifeblood from two young schoolgirls
Intending to destroy their whole world
A pervert ever alert as to who he could hurt
Animals and children were his two targets
Gaining a killer's skill with an evil swipe
His practice followed the mass-archetype
A vulnerable victim's life one to be wiped

However harsh one we cannot avoid or ignore
As their cruelty strikes our humanity's core
Serial killers who murdered on the loose
Became an artisan and craftsman criminal
Honing their heart moving from hand to eye
Trading every life for a lie upon a lie
First practised their skill on animal-after-animal

A Living Prize

The boy threw the hoop
And caught a fish in the dish
His aim led to his claim
The stallholder handed the happy child
A plastic bag holding a trapped goldfish

The farmer edged destitution
Needed to give his life a lift
The charity collected restitution
Then bought him a tethered goat
They gave him as a lifetime gift

The answer to all her prayers
Needed to survive right now
Something to plough the field
A forced creature for a future yield
The charity gave her a burdened cow

Yet the cow and goat and goldfish
Will make them poor rather than rich
For each one will take more water
Even before they are slaughtered
When the real gift is plain to see
To irrigate the land so plants are free

Cultivate passion for work in the field
Compassion as our sword and shield

The future plan for the land
Serves to ruin time's sand
Only cultivates a mass cruelty

To deprive the fish of the sea
To confine a goat to misery
To force a cow to be a standee
The present reflects our future
Creating a problem plain to see
Careful cultivation of any society
Needs more than organically obtuse
Our mores built on an altar of abuse
Their future and yours depends on you
Reversing our role as nature's cuckoo

A Number minus a Name

The Chinese seek science without sleaze
As parthogenesis is practical in the lab
In 2022 the 220 mice embryos were tested
Of them 219 were wasted and infested
Nameless on every discarded carcass

The South Koreans eat a hearty meal
Not caring for his last pleading squeal
As 1½ million dogs a year are beaten
Their flesh is tender ready to be eaten
No name on the menu for their carcass

In the UK the contused pigs are killed
Brexit butchers were in short supply
So 35,000 pigs were simply slaughtered
With their bodies left to rot in a land fill
No name on the dead killed at our will

The UK victims are incinerated in chains
Turned upside down in the metal frame
Then their throats slit with a honed machete
90 million are killed every year for religion
Religious ritual slaughter is never exhausted
Adding suffering on death of each hung carcass
As our acceptable face of an animal holocaust

In America the KKK found each black victim
Then took photographs of each tortured face
Lynchings numbered over 12,000 in 12 States
In their rancid hearts and jammed moral cogs
Along with black people they hanged 4000 dogs

Alas victims were dismissed with common sass
Nameless in a redneck circus as a lynched carcass
A name signifies an identity in society
So no need of a name for an animal slave
Framed to be a number by you and me
Whose death is all that sets them free

A Panther with a Panther

In 2022 in downtown Brunswick city
Their acts resonate without pity
Ahmaud Arbery was hunted
Three men beneath cold stars
Tracked him in revving cars
Strapped in by their trap
Travis McMichael held him
Too close with his loaded shotgun
Outnumbered with nowhere to run
Shot three times at close range
His chest blown away by the blast
In seconds Ahmaud breathed his last

Ahmaud was part of their jape
So one thing was for certain
Their trophy behind the curtain
With no need for a crystal ball
To see he would never escape
Downed by McMichael's bullets
Finger poised on the trigger
An itching honky pulled it
One two three burst bullets
Ahmaud fell as a poacher's victim
Ahmaud's life skimmed on their rim
Caught by their bias and vigour and vim
In the night justice grew dim outside him

Month after month passed without arrest
While the three hunters escaped justice
Ahmaud was not one the cops missed
Doing nothing was their practised bliss

Self-defence became McMichael's claim
Indeed a justice card was the trio's game
They had no intent to hurt him or maim
He was a stranger they saw on the street
Figured he was some unwelcome dead-beat
They followed tracking his pounding feet
Paced him moving to their own drumbeat
He had no chance to flee let alone retreat
In an instant he had no heartbeat
Blood flowed from his head and feet
A problem was their lies were liquid
The video showed what they had hid
Dylan wisely noted with no guile
'Look out kid, it's somethin' you did'
With a D.A on his track and their style
Meant the killing had to end in a trial

McMichael squirmed as the questions
Demanded answers on his sworn oath
Half answered with truth's indigestion
All he was asked was too tough a task
Then again when being cross-examined
Hung on hooks by an advocate sleuth
McMichael found no escape route
Ahmaud in reverse in their pursuit
They could not find lies to refute
Caught by the questing law's claws
A single unassailable nailed truth

The judge was fixed in his sentence
'Life' for the one they had taken
The same one for each of the three
Now serving time in the penitentiary

While young Arbery spends his time
In a mahogany overcoat for their crime
Six feet below in a cold earth cemetery
It was Bobby Seale's oft cited claim
Black men were white men's fair game
From Ahmaud Arbery to George Floyd
Remains the same of a life destroyed
A line that stilled the life of Emmett Till
Is a soiled memory that lingers forever
Finger-pointing at killers as lawgivers
In the flowing Medger Evers river
Their rednecks and their clan
See black people as criminals
To be accused and abused
Then held in a roped noose
Much as we see all animals
To be abused and used
Being amused for our use
Never let loose without an excuse

Their clan strung up the dog too
Proof what they knew to be true
A philosophy borne of warped pride
A black man and his dog side-by-side
Each noose a different kind of caboose
On the wrong end of the crowded train
Yet the feeling induced was the same
Animal or black on a one-way track

The deal between the panthers
Is a question hunters never ask
They move with a defined rancour
For the panther and black panther

To them is just the same
Prejudice is their anchor
A politician's swivel-eyed shame
Rely on us to play a crooked game

A Pigment of their Imagination

On 9 March 2022
An anonymous scientist cried
When the man whose heart
He replaced suddenly died
While the pig whose heart
Was stolen for scientific pride
Has long been quietly cast aside
Another acrid statistic incinerated
Her science lab history recorded
Only a number without a name
Their interest long ago evaporated
Her present represents her past
A foreigner from another caste
A lab sample never meant to last

On May Day 2022 they checked the DNA
As to why the experiment failed that day
They found the animal they killed
The pig whose life they stilled
In order to steal her heart away
Had been stricken with a virus
From her forebears in a wet market
So the pig they used to fire us
With zeal for ending her life

Claiming a miracle by saving his life
Had been our victim who died twice
Dying first as we pleased
Dying again from our disease
Each time as we the public planned
Far from being a miracle of science
She was killed at will by a scalpel hand

A Pope and a Pet

The Pope sermonizing for our redemption
Claimed 'couples who choose to forego
Children and prefer pets are selfish'
Perhaps why religion abhors angelfish
For he should know as one in the know
Who subscribes to the story of a starfish
Is an admission no need to parry a priest
In a religion whose priests do not procreate
Though they are happy to orally vibrate
Renaming parenthood he claimed
'Takes away your humanity'
Failing to see what promotes poverty
On a tightrope balanced by missal inanity
Between profundity and priest-led profanity
His no dope-false hope of an idea
Springs from a notion of Vatican vanity

His religion is focused on a falsehood foxhole
Only humans matter as only humans have a soul
From half-baked ideas of Aristotle
All were void and devoid of bottle
To a prejudiced virus honed by Aquinas
A theory based on an idea with a hollow whole
Perfect progress to drag religion into the 21st century
Adopting a rescued cat or dog or any stray animal
Would show the meaning of common humanity
Perhaps if he helped any abandoned animal to cope
Maybe the Pope would be practising Christianity

In his vast wealthy world in the richest place
The Pope fails to find a welcome space

For the homeless and the abused children
As well as our countless abused animals
Whose lives have all been unfurled
While he parades in his privileged world
They seek nothing more than a passion
Of humility and a mite from St Francis
Delivering the kissed riches of compassion

Priests without children with evil intent
Are content to loiter outside the tent
Then hide behind the beguiled smile
Of the prancing practised paedophile
It is little wonder lest he forgets
A reason some people prefer pets
Rather than stare into his religious abyss
How much wiser he would prove to be
Following the teaching of St Francis
Who saw the church as cause and effect
Of so much avoidable animal misery
Spreading his message wider than Assisi
So much better than another red letter
From the privileged poise of one who can
Find odd succour behind the gilded walls
Where valuable paintings hang in the halls
No eyes see the battered homeless woman
No thoughts given to the forgotten tarpan

Christian Brothers and nuns in Ireland
Abused the children because they could
Killed the baby and destroyed the mother
To a woman and a man because they can
Then in Canada for over 100 years
Truth grabbed at birth and smothered

The Pope visits to offer a pious apology
To the Indians enslaved at five-years-old
The abused in mind and body and heart
By religious zealots ripping them apart
Hearing they were no different than a buffalo
Added another kind of abuse to their woe
When the Chiefs heard his words 'I apologise'
They recognised the impact of imported lies

A starving dog barks at the departing caravan
A poverty of morality forced by one who can
Imposed on the universe by one in the Vatican
Pius XII agreed with Hitler to hide the priests
Who abused children and then fled to the East
Meanwhile today another choirboy is defiled
Hidden from the public and any prying eyes
Priest perverts abuse another defenceless child
The problem is so near and yet so clear
Could be seen by any passing blind beggar
In a skip-rescued broken Vatican mirror

A Procrustean Apology

All say 'sorry' as if a politician's plea
Meaning I hope you'll feel sorry for me
For where principle counts for nothing
All lies can be sold and bought
I would not have dreamed of uttering
Some useless or pointless apology
Except for the fact that 'I was caught'

Could be that fat creep Elliott
Who laughed drain-style of course
Sitting astride a sad-eyed laid-out horse
Who could not move a muscle or his head
The obese creep knew she was already dead

Mickey Todd was an abusive sod
Who whipped and whipped a horse
With branches he grabbed in a temper
Struck the horse who faltered at the water
Todd did not care as it was only a horse
Who had in her time won him slight fame
And even a good name at least until now
As day becomes night he became a knight
As any other politician who dishes the dirt
Not caring who or why someone was hurt
Unless he hit her in a tempered curse
A victim who could not resist such force
Ideally a frightened spooked whipped horse

At Madox Farm workers caught on camera
Bullying pride they did not even try to hide
A Zouma kick to a cow in the belly and chest

45

They raised another by a hoist from her rest
Then smacked one in the face with a spade
Because the cow was too scared to move
Though who and why of those were savage
Was plain to see it is these farm workers
Who could be you or worse or all of us

Forget the foolish plea to forget
The animals and just 'move on'
That is no answer at all then or now
To the abused cat or horse or cow
Who might now be dead and gone

With the sincerity of a politician
They make a pointless repetition
They stretch their Procrustean bed
Robber liars whose muddled head
In and out of Parliament is spent
Finding excuses then twisted and bent
Selling us a second-rate insincerity
To try to fool the public and society
They offer deception that is never bought
We know their delivery adds up to nought
Abuse by bullies and cowards is self-taught
Never ever apologising for their onslaught
From the camera and letter and tape
Moving every which way to find an escape
However dressed up the words always sought
Hide that they mean 'I'm sorry I was caught'

A Queen's Gambit

The Russian looked at his opponent
Who stared back in slick disdain
Concealed hate under the counter
One lived without a brand of liberty
One kissed the stone of democracy
As each played their secret game
The American looked at his opponent
His eyes betraying his hatred
Each detested everything about the other
Each saw brainwashing as truth smothered
Their ideals paraded stark naked
For him democracy was sacred
The Russian and American traded
Their silent thoughts and ideals
Yet no one there
None who watched
Even knew or even cared
How the one who stares
As the centre of their game
Whose life was pawned
Without a stifled yawn
For her shining curved horn
A used stooge with no name
They neither figured the figure
Sliced limbs cracked and hacked
A life taken by a poacher's trigger
Her body blasted to smithereens
On the one-way track block
So a lie is spawned in hock
While lies are hooked and lame
Her tusk shaped as a tactile queen

The pawn in our life-long game
Those whose minds quicken
Notice the neatly carved piece
Of one whose life was fleeced
Her pain vibrates percussion
By an American and a Russian
A visible elephant in the room
A pawn followed by our spume
Her tusk as our new age tomb
A death determined in her womb
A life stolen as the poacher sang
A life ended in her shared pang
A silent clang of our zugzwang

A Shark in shallow Waters

Into the shallow water
The huge troubled fish sailed on
His fin was broken
His body was shot
His race was run
He floated in shock
His blow-hole was blocked

All the people gathered around
When they heard the pained sound
Of the foreign creature they found
Bobbing through the surface sea
As he struggled on the quicksand
They moved closer as a band
Intending to lend a helping hand

He had been injured and knocked
He was bleeding and land-locked

Although he was distressed and all alone
The people figured with their help
He would soon be on his way home

People multiplied to make sure he did not die
Vets and cast nets and the cranes and the planes
All gathered to rescue the massive bleeding fish
From the trapped dish of sinking sand
As his life was being swiftly extinguished

When finally after sweat and toil
Of days and days on end

Their effort came to the boil
People on the quayside and pier
Shouted and clapped and cheered
When the giant was set free
To sail on home into the inviting sea

Ropes were removed so he could sway
With the sparkling ship as his guide
Lest he became prey to a nomad shark
As the sea left him nowhere to hide
The wide-eyed ship sailed alongside
As the wary Star Chamber sailors
Helped him towards his home
Yet he looked weary and so alone

Out of sight of the shore
The sailors spoke to each other
Then gave a knowing nod
That was readily understood
Though there was no pod
One would be enough for today
It would satisfy the glinted eye
Of the search and research
All in the name of science
They loaded a fancy appliance

Out of sight of those waving from the shore
Time was running out and they had to score

His bleeding pleading eyes met theirs
They were busy with their own affairs
His silent plea seemed lost in the surging sea

As the appliance was unsheathed
The huge fish no longer breathed
As the ship that had rescued him
Unveiled the Star Chamber flag
Then all too soon
Beneath the freezing moon
They took the giant's life
By their honed harpoon
Through the swirling sea they fled
Leaving the ocean clothed in red
With blood and blubber and body
Spread on the ship's bed
His colour matched their masthead

Research was a tag they used with ease
Covering every kind of known disease
Research was a word they used for lies
Keeping truth hidden from prying eyes
As if research was an infectious disease
Though in the main a variety of greed
The sailors and crew did as they pleased
Not caring one iota about foreign legalese
For the harpoon-laden ship was Japanese

A Spotless Life

Mary Smith gazed out the window
Her heart was hit with a warm glow
The feeling even lit her face aglow
Seeing the first shoots rise in spring
The new-born lamb gambolling free
Such a sight made her lone soul sing
She ate at the restaurant every day
During her quiet week-long stay
Quite taken with the spotted lamb
The same one she swiftly recognised
Same time same place every day
He had a black spot between his eyes
The little lamb put on a daily display
As if pleased to be seen by her at play
Jumping and looking cutely at Mary
She smiled back without being chary
Straightaway he made her happy day
Then she was hooked in time's flow
Smith packed her bags ready to go
Still keen to see her cute little lamb
She spotted him among all the rams
At play in their gambolling programme
But then when she took a closer look
Smith instantly knew she was wrong
The black spot was in the wrong place
On the cutest lamb's still smiley face
Smith was anxious during the new day
Still worried she caught a waiter's attention
Even after a short stay in her quiet way
It was something she just had to mention
She was feeling kind of slightly bereft

She hopped nervously before she left
Whim wham she asked about the lamb
The waiter too shifted from foot to foot
The waiter seemed more than confused
Shook his head as if he had no words
Except those he knew to make her grieve
Yet now if ever was not the time to deceive
He knew those who do not lead spotless lives
Should still be able to deliver and be believed
The waiter held his steady steely gaze
Softly catching her eyes in a dull blaze
Yet the waiter was not one easily fazed
The cogs in his mind started to crunch
Not sure how to say it but he had a hunch
Delivered a kick as hard as a blacksmith's blow
Much as Judy's well-aimed rolling pin on Punch
'Why the one with the black spot between his eyes
Was the same one you munched for your lunch'

A Trophy for Vanity

Proudly she stands with her foot
On the head of her prey
Her weapon across her shoulder
The trophy for a well-paid day
A handsome reward for the risk
She takes on every shoot
For the victim could fight back
And deprive her of the loot
She smiles so the photograph
Will capture the unleashed iron
That coursed through her
When she sees her bagged lioness
Or better still the shaggy lion
Adding another notch on her bedpost list
The feeling of power too hard to resist
Yet she fails to see through her vanity mist
The ghost of her image turned topsy-turvy
Her phoney claim to be a 'conservationist'
Cuts a tarnished symbol as some women see
The trophy hunter as naked as a naturist
The trophy hunter as nature's terrorist
The trophy killer as a stalking rapist

The rapist steals a piece of his victim
Sings his hymn of hate as a maxim
To take away as a token of his prey
To dwell on his perverts power
Used to slay the one in the way
A perfect reminder of his crime
A mirror-image of his victim
A trophy of power that satisfies him

A rapist and trophy hunter whose vanity
Advertises a naked hatred of humanity

A Whale of a Time

When you take the life of a whale
With a strike that explodes inside
You can feel his pain in Braille
When you see that spouting fountain
And the magic of that sea mountain
As he glides through the ocean
And you get the shared notion
To follow where he leads
And make sure he bleeds
Beneath the beauty of a cold moon
Only darkened by the boon
Of a hot hammered harpoon

Do not blame me I am only the captain
I just follow orders
Across all the borders
Sweeping the seven seas
Doing what others ask of me
When I set sail
I risk the gale
Out on the trail
Follow their wail
There is no avail
Of their travail
I am here to deliver a whale

Do not blame me I am only a sailor
Trying to make a living
Taking all that the whale's giving
A modern Jack Tar it is true
Doing what I am told to do

We cannot afford to fail
We are there just to nail
His flashing tail
The real tell-tale
I will assail
Of their travail
I am here to deliver the whale

Do not blame me I am only a buyer
Looking for a profit
How much I can make off it
When the competition is rife
Letting them make a good life
They are just part of the retail
When their weapons impale
The capture of the whale
No more bail
Monitor the flail
Of their travail
I am here to deliver the whale

Do not blame me I am only the customer
Wanting another tasty meal
At a price that is the best deal
His death gives me hope
As I love soap on a rope
The smell I have to inhale
I do not want it stale
Or their gaol
Only the sale
With no bail
Of their travail
I am here to devour the whale

Together we have all aided
Economies we have braided
Then there is the side-line
When the whale is mine
And the wails of the whales
No reason for blackmail
No different than a foxtail
It is off the scale
Getting a giant male
Draw the veil
Of their travail
We are here to deliver the whale

Catching him sharpens our soul jaded by life
We do not fuss too much about any wildlife
We just trust in the thrust of our explosive knife

You are looking at it
From the wrong direction
We do it from pure affection
See the swishing tail
Hear her bellowing wail
As the harpoon explodes
Our heads are in overload
If it is female
If it is frail
We do not quail
Of their travail
We are here to deliver the whale

You have to understand
That at sea or on land
Everything changes and rearranges

For you and me our destiny is planned
After all he has had his time
It is now time to call it quits
He has lived in our shadow
For far too long
And we are here
To make sure his inside splits
We catch them when the sea sprays their wine
That is why we caught him in his peak-prime
Everyone has a whale of a time
It is not as if we commit a crime
The rhythm of the seas is our rhyme
After all until the moment she is caught
Even the whale has a great time
Like a lover in life's race
She too enjoys the chase
You should see her smiling face
She knows there is no escape
From the whaler's intent to rape
We take her out in a bloody blaze
A smile a harpoon could not erase

Without a wish to cause them any strife
It is a natural part of them being wildlife
Their price for living is paid by our knife

So shake the dice and toss a coin
We will decide which one to purloin
Hold tight and gird your loin
You might get the chance to join

When you are a giant among men
It is a thrill when we wreak our will

A thrill we share when we kill
There is no fancy word to add to a frill
Much like your pet with his prey
Getting her in our grip makes our day
That is a bill that is always a winterkill
Truth's tart pill is best told by the shrill
Of the lone whippoorwill
Believe me there is no substitute
For the fire inside when you shoot
Is our gain as her pain is mute
We are intent on stealing her loot
We all walk tall wearing a jackboot

A Woman and a Hat and a Black Cat

Flames licked her feet
Fire burned her limbs
Screaming with confused innocence
Prayer and prejudice were the twins
Mixed as one as the fire flew high
Her soul sold by stone-hearted strangers
Her fortune fixed by biased neighbours
Under a crescent moon and a starless sky

Flames locked her face
Scorched her pale wrinkled skin
Her eyes burned by fiery guilt
Her skeleton cursed by mortal sin
A neighbour cabal saw fit to light a fuse
Beneath her broken body born to lose
Our history with a reason for the Blues
A suspect truth proved as a social ruse

Whatever was a trumped up reason
As always never mattered too much
As long as we could burn another woman
Left without a friend or funds or a crutch
For good measure throw her in a dirt-ridden ditch
No cemetery sermon for a woman branded a witch
So the lies die on her tongue as no truth could tell
We grabbed her broomstick and hat and cat as well
Lest his magnetic green eyes
Would remind us of our lies
No memory of our bias could survive
Her companion cat staked by her side

All's well so our victims could end well
Their future forged when our prejudice fell
Burned and buried in our earthbound hell

The burning glowed from Essex to Salem
A country and century separated them
Discovered its target across tide and time
Find a vulnerable victim to use and condemn
The witch's cat is an ideal victim to abuse
Proves our reason for a raging ruse to use
Other lives we choose as to who will lose
Black defines the woman her cat and her hat
Burned on the anvil of our biased eye-tooth
We need no evidence when we run out of ruth
Our power of prejudice stands the test of time
A power without reason as a substitute for truth

A Zoonotic Reservoir

Follow the zoonotic river
From an animal reservoir
That flows and grows in the ruin
That drew in
Every creature
That flew in
The air around Wuhan
That grew in
The water around Wuhan
They slew in
The fields around Wuhan
Where the crew in
The Virology Institute
Avoid the truth by a mute response
To the question everyone wants
To know
Which they rue in
And let the world
Stew in
While the river stills flows
While the sludge grows
While the reservoir cries
While the river still dies
While the wildlife
Brew in
While the world sleeps
While the world weeps
Tears with no limit in size
Martyrdom versus our panjandrum
Beneath the barbaric Beijing skies

Albert Went Hunting

Albert learned while young
The value of violence in bud
Climbing the ladder's first rung
Witnessed his father's manhood
The lesson of his childhood
Black eyes and blotched blood
Seeing his mother assaulted
Her beating was never halted
A daily act Albert understood
As a joy seeing someone stung
One-by-one he broke her fingers
Used his strength in sober anger
Albert grew his bitter hunger
A father's legacy for a son
Seeking gain with pain on the run
For his waking slow-burn future
To find a perfect victim to attack
Someone too weak to fight back
Using strength as a wavelength
For his masculine aphrodisiac

Albert trapped stray cats and dogs
Locked in crates and easy to flog
His dead heart turned his head cogs
Shooting arrows tipped with hate
Into the howling wailing crates
Sent his head and heart reeling
Creating their fear-filled feeling
A heightened pleasure with no ceiling
Creatures growing as mounting prey
Slowly tortured by him day after day

Abusing victims became his leisure
No limit pain measure on measure
A jaundiced eye ignited a spark
He tried to satisfy by do-or-die
Fixed on who to violate
Searching for a victim of hate
By chance he discovered her
With lies and ties he deceived her
His power craving put her in peril
Albert broke her body and her will

From one to a thousand women
Each one his chosen perfect victim
Honed by a stone heart and ice-pick whim
The art of torture his first resort
A psychologist J. Brussell told the court
'Albert went hunting that was his thing'
Killing primed his mind's mainspring
Like the fox and stag and trophy hunter
Abuse as a self-appointed raptor
Any selected woman's age and appearance
Neither mattered nor magnetised him
Power alone was his verve and vim
A lonely woman or a crated animal
A feckless thrill without any trammel
No difference as a random reference
Albert's victim changed
Each by type and name
Yet their ID remained the same

A cat and a dog unto death in a crate
An 80-year-old woman on his summon

A dead body or carcass of a victim
All caught by his creed of murderous fate

Hate and love vying as a lifelong twin
So strong in him no victim could win

Albert ravished and murdered many women
Each life suspended as he determined
Each life then ended as he determined
Each one another volunteer specimen
Their future flowed through his finger's sand
As their executioner he planned his demands
Much as a shark caught on a tensioned line
Turns towards his death by a terrorist angler
Proud of his power while their lives dangled
Albert was a one-man criminal killing band
Albert sprayed each life as a tainted spangler
Tossed and twisted by their tormented tangler
Used a stiletto to slit his victim's throat
He saw a woman as his sacrificial goat
Veins pumped when their pain made him gloat
A victim's zugzwang life lassoed by a wrangler
A muscle memory kept him alive and afloat
De Salvo went hunting as The Boston Strangler

Animalhood in the Hood

Palms were laid down as alms
To reach us perhaps to teach us
With no intent to preach to us
Simply showing what was true
A sign neither warped nor wonky
Okay for her to arrive by a donkey
So it is good enough for you too

Yet of all the animals that are used
She is whipped for being too slow
When the burden is much too heavy
When the burden is too much to bear
Then the lazy owner whips her more
Knowing no one notices her burden
Even worse he knows no one cares

Whip and whip and whip until his knuckles bleed
Lash on lash for his own growing greed over need
The mule is lashed as a spreading violent cancer
Where the ass and donkey and mule is the best
Weakest victim so a whip is always the answer

Meanwhile the heat of the desert sun
Burns down upon her scarred back
Her hangnail hooves and arthritic joints
She flinches when he beats her with a crupper
The profit-laden owner is good and ready
To reward her service and repay past deeds
So he hacks her up as an amateur butcher
To offer her to the customer as a last supper

Christmas Day in care is always a sad and bleak affair
Yet for any animal awaiting a visit by a human cannibal
From birth it is Christmas Day anywhere and everywhere
Spanked and split by whips that cut through bone to blood
In some form every single one no less than a valueless scud
Compassion as our creed buried deep beneath the cold mud
Past present and future plight of all animalhood in the hood
An epitaph flag unfurls in our world as their neighbourhood
Showing the crested chaff as a symbol for all animalhood

Animals Circling Space

A dog smiles with handcuffed teeth
Fixed with a grinding induced fear
Facing death without a wreath
Her gaping mouth forced open
Struck in shock with a silent scream

The rocket hurtles in a slipstream
A black heart hole of hollow space
Her confusion on our fusion scheme
Is etched deep on her panicked face
Her nightmare living our idle dream

Round and round for a million miles
A dog replaced by a manacled monkey
Still fixed with his death-mask smile
A volunteer exhibit is found and bound
Twisted through our master race turnstile

The scientists claim their honours
Then bask in the glory and fame
Though the dog and monkey fades
No experimenter knew their name
For that would mean an identity
As they sail in our sad space sea
Sailing forever in a cloudy future
A black hole serves as a ligature
Circling for us as a stoned Sisyphus
Caught between science and society
Expendable objects in our space race
A shooting star of man-made misery

A small step for mankind
A false step as a blind-side
A one-way trip to Mars
A trip to the marred stars
A lottery ticket for a life
A life of pure trumpery
A loss we win by usury
Laika a stray mongrel stolen on a Moscow street
Forced to circle the earth under a callous moon
She died terrified inside a Russian rocket at Noon
Laika a sacrifice in six hours for a science perjury
Animals handcuffed to our shallow space sorcery

Arms Are Meant To Hold You

The diner considered he was a culinary expert
Bored and tired of eating average food
He wanted something to excite his jaded palate
He opened a restaurant with a great deal of fuss
With a tank full of fish of every description
Though the main exotic offer was an octopus
He was so inventive he called it 'Octopie'
He intended to pluck the creature from the tank
Hack off her arms to watch her slowly die
Then place her on his plate
As that was to be her fate
Swiftly become part of the diner's face
He looked as happy as a sandman
At least that was his plain plan
When they sat down and quietly waited
When he plucked the octopus out
They licked their lips waiting to be plated
Then truth to tell he slipped
Then stumbled and fell pell-mell
The octopus reached and grabbed his neck
Suddenly in seconds he was held by an arm
Then two and all eight of them
Each springing from their body stem

Eight arms in a stranglehold so tight
He could barely begin to put up a fight
The more he struggled the tighter the grip
There was no slip betwixt the cup and lip
As the octopus caught his bulging eyes
A choice in the moment could be realised
Presented to him by the diner's cute fall

To win the fight in a final choice all in all
The expert spread out across the floor
Sheepish diners slipped out the door
Seeing the predator had eight arms
Was enough to resist her charms
Although he had wanted no fuss
That was what he got because
It was a one-sided ruckus
Though a lot of them cussed
Most never bothered to visit the restaurant again
The most they did was attend his funeral in the rain
Indeed no one there tried to eat any octopus again

Baby Fae and the Baboon

The baboon did not have a name
Her only claim to fame
Was as part of an end game
Scientists grabbed her from the cage
Then set the instruments as a gauge
When her body was breaking
Then her heart was taken
When everyone except the baboon
Was engaged at each bloody stage
For an experiment of a high order
As they broke into a new border
A frontier with no veneer of a tear
One that had never been tried before
Then again remember it was in 1984

In time it was the saddest of sad days
When Baby Fae finally lost her fight
Even the vivisectors were in a daze
When they tried in vain to analyse
Why the experiment did not go right
Especially when all of it was in sight
As they dwelt upon her sorry plight
The baboon's body shunted out the door
As with the last one and the one before
But we should remember that was 1984

Baby Fae is remembered as one
Who was at the frontier of science
Something failed in an appliance
A baboon's heart as a misalliance
Alas no success to serenade

Even now the sadness still pervades
The minds of those on parade
Used a baboon in a masquerade
Scientists tried against the odds
To save a child survive life's rod
As it should be her name is known
By the scientists and the world
For we need to know the child
Did not die in vain
By recalling her name
Each time a scientist fights for a life
Each baby's survival on another day
Will follow a lodestar set by Baby Fae
So we can remember it was in 1984
The baboon never left the room
She was scientifically groomed
As a neo-child in a cage to perform
Her last act on an experimental stage
No one at all could recall her name
No one could remember her number
Then again why should they anyway

There was no reason before or now
When following science's holy cow
All that matters is what happens
Behind each secret locked door
The supposed prescience of science
As a talismanic manifest alliance
Slavery is freedom and peace is war
An idea borrowed straight out of Orwell
So we can dwell on our truth pell-mell
When our key opens their cell

Strikes each hour as their death-bell
Time immemorial until the next knell

For animals in 2022 at death's door
A science score of a science whore
The sound of statistics drowned
A science score for a science whore
Animal experiments as more encores
Heroes and victims of our man-of-war
In 2024 it was is and will be a turnstile 1984

Black is the Colour

Agnes Waterhouse was feared by neighbours
Attacked as anti-social in her labours
Keeping herself-to-herself they levelled at her
As a crime when all she wanted was no favours
Happy to live on her own terms
Agnes stood firm and never squirmed
Agnes was her own woman
Agnes was made of tough stuff
Agnes refused to turn for the worms
The neighbours burned her to death
Then to be sure they found 500 more
So their black arts soul would be rived
Before fully burned they were cut down
One by one they were buried alive
So a single woman would not survive

Agnes had few friends and no funds
A community of cautious black cats
A couple who wore pointed black hats

Villagers had free rein to practise prejudice
For the biased cynics their pain cut no ice
Agnes and her black cat were burned in a pack
The rest was a smokescreen and a smokestack
Then thrown together into the freshly dug pit
Using joint hate as their neighbourly template
Screeching bodies of the squirming black cats
Fighting death as the soil covered their noses
The Essex people went about their business
Tending graves with sweet smelling pink roses

Marking the graves of the ones who died
People's prejudice burned bright with pride

A woman screamed yet no one heard her
A woman against neighbours who hurt her
A black cat against the ones who burnt her
A woman with a black cat meets prejudice
A woman with reason enough for all of us
A woman and cat condemned due to colour
A woman and a cat hanged by the jugular
A woman with a black cat without purdah
A woman worthy of our past resort to murder
A woman alone is a target for a cop to murder

An animal and a woman without a girder
Has no protection from those who herd her
Abusers use a victim as a slur for their spur
After 400 years they view Agnes and her cat
Through the same skewed vision of a voyeur

Blank Heart of a Hunter

I remember the pure thrill of the kill
The sheer rush that shot through my veins
When I looked and saw your ruddy remains
I had to quickly turn away

Though I still feel the fun of that first kill
There's a difference I hate to confess
Today in some way I first saw death's mess
And knew you are no different to me

All I recall is the hell of it all
When I looked deep into your eyes
And at once I counted how many lies
I still continue to tell myself

I was blooded by my dad as a cub
And I felt important that day
Yet what I know is the real rub
Since then I have lived a lie
In every way in what I do and say

Blind Faith/Blind Justice

Barrels of their blood and buckets of gore
Deep offal swill seeps under the door
Leave the stun gun 'cause you're in control
Cut out their hearts 'cause they've got no soul
The upturned cattle bleed over the floor
While greedy leaders plead for an encore
Shouting 'more, more, more' for profits galore
Hear the repertoire of your warm abattoir

Follow blind faith so they fail to see
Mock blind justice and make slaves of the free

You slaughter a creature you slaughter God
Fire the wire of the electric prod
While the chained cow writhes in the wired cage
Then slit her throat when she roars with rage
Then watch her drown slowly in bubbling blood
As her pain-stained face spurts a fountain flood
As you perform your ritual slaughter
A rite written in blood but writ in water

The new-born calf torn from her mother
Reminds Isaac of his long-lost mother
The calf sucks the slaughter man's fingers
The smell of her mother's fear lingers
All she drinks is the milk of human vice
His knife ends her life from his heart of ice
Calf and child cries through the eyes of Singer
Each mother forced through the gates of Treblinka

How we treat animals, the Nazi's treated us.
Are you on the side of the angels or Judas?

Bathsheba betrayed by one who bought her
Isaac knew her fate when they caught her
Nazis refused to give any quarter
Lined her up for their ritual slaughter
Memories of his mother's tattooed stamp
As Bathsheba was gassed in Herr Hitler's camp

Isaac Singer was a Jew
Who knew what was true
Saw ritual slaughter as a pale excuse
A dressed up disguise of animal abuse
Singer shot truth's arrow as the clincher
Catching the zealots hook, line and sinker:
To animals we are all Nazi's
And for them it's an eternal Treblinka

Blue-bird sings the Blues

She flew through the unchained
Sky-blue countryside
Sparkling eyes and freedom's song
Spiralling and soaring wide
Twists and turns as nature's acrobat
On a wild glide wing
Her timeless tune is proof
The blue-bird was born to sing

A single shot from the one with a sawn-off soul
A single shot burst out to end her timed life's toll
A single shot in spring split her pain-filled sighs
Blasted the last blue-bird from the blood-spilled skies

On her wing lies the bleeding shotgun bruise
In her eyes lies the stark dark spark of her muse
At once her shattered heart proves who to accuse
Denied her silvery voice leaves her no choice
Silently the dead-eyed blue-bird sings the Blues

Blues for Charlie Hebdo

The teacher committed the final crime
He dared to ridicule a religion
Not just any old stool pigeon
As in pornography or Christianity
Or some odd Seventh Day Adventist
The type of eternal optimist

The teacher committed the sacred crime
As the bells of Rhymney chime
With a doom-laden sound
As Samuel Paty is remembered
For being dismembered by some zealot
Thinking they have a monopoly on truth
When they can issue a crass fatwa
Who can hound a man to death
Who can stone a woman to death
Who can claim it is such a religion
And then kill animals in a cruel ruse
The barbaric ritual slaughter
That is simply animal abuse
Dressed up as a religious excuse

Think of the profit in ritually killing an animal
Forget the victim as it is much more subliminal
Search for a false ritual to find the real criminal
As they want to please their palate
And it is only a bleeding animal
When it bellows as it bleeds to death
Upside down on the abattoir floor
A notch below a woman
A pace behind a camel

Their lives are untrammelled
As killing is their business
In the name of religion
So another day writ in water
With the mathematics multiplying
The profits gained by ritual slaughter
They figure they have a monopoly on truth
Yet you do not have to be any kind of sleuth
Seeing them hide behind a robe and mask
Without being asked and gives a sign
Saying you remind me of the blind lawyer
Searching for a defence dressed as a reason
While trying to avoid a true charge of treason

Finally the prophet asked about Pilate
Who posed the question 'What is truth?'
Then had the grace to save face by walking away
Unlike you whose values follow the false muse
To use abuse as a religious ruse
Then drink the water of oblivion
The prophet declared kindness to all beings
With eyes seeing no need for the greed
Of the voyeur and the Greek poseur
Showing less bottle than biased Aristotle
As everyone who follows a religion
That devalues animals as their property
Intent on using their quirky zeal
To throttle free speech and liberty

All religions advocate kindness to animals
To practice abuse is just a religious excuse
Whatever rite and ruse they may try to use
Reason is not delivered by a bludgeon

Anymore than violence as their oxygen
It is time to sing Charlie Hebdo's Blues
As an unchained charter we can use
To fight for the right to be free from abuse
Whether she is a pangolin or a pachyderm
She is born to live on her own terms
Charlie Hebdo explored the vestibule
Of ideas as a straight moral rule
No religion is immune from ridicule
Whether delivered by a genius or a fool
Charlie Hebdo delivered a spool
Of truth in their cartoon panorama
Like the great and good in Tell Mama
Terrorists' lies shattered by Faith Matters
The silence of treason dealt a blow
Their vigilance clearing the cesspool
By the sign of Westergaard and Hebdo
Using truth as their tale-telling tool

Blues for Harriet Tubman

Araminta Ross watched the burning cross
While her name flickered in the flame
When her Master sold her body
To Massa whose cruelty flowed through his veins
So she vowed to break the chains
Forged by law and stamped by birth
She broke them all and escaped on the run
To prove to the world her true worth

Up North she became Harriet Tubman
Risked her life in the Deep South
Saving slaves down in Maryland
Condemned to death from every Slavers' mouth
Each saved slave marked out her grave
A bounty placed on her head
Didn't stop her rescuing fugitives
Though the Slavers wanted her dead

Harriet beat them one and all
Living and fighting for freedom
Then died when she was 93
They placed her face on an American stamp
No longer cast as a runaway scamp
She became the face of black history

So can you measure the distance for me
It's so dark here I can hardly see
I'm blinded by the light of law and our history

Emmilene Pankhurst stepped beyond the law
When she hurled a cobbled stone

Through the Prime Minister's window
Sending the Suffragettes signed message home
They became State enemies
Force-fed women in prison
Pankhurst became one more human *foie gras*
To destroy her and her vision

Louise Hageby followed in the same vein
Her freedom fight fuelled by rage
She saw the plight of her sisters
The same as victims in a scientist's cage
They saw the law was used
In the cruel 'Brown Dog Affair'
They smashed the shambles of a science lab
To show the Government they cared

They fought the police in the streets
Then they torched the Gardens at Kew
Tube-fed by force they died and roared
Until the Government released them all
Freed from their cell they could enter the Hall
Then got what they fought for by a World War

So can you measure the distance for me
It's so dark here I can hardly see
I'm blinded by the light of law and our history

Ronnie Lee lived and worked in the law
For those facing a sentence
Serving the feckless and reckless
Seeking justice while they paid their penance
He aimed to support the weak
Their tongue often in a knot

Sometimes trying to prove their innocence
So they're not in a cell to rot

Then his sense of 'what is justice' shifted
When he saw the law was grim
Treating those who were different
Yet in many ways they were just like him
Looking in his cracked mirror
Figured they too should be free
As a lawyer he formed the A.L.F.
A beacon for their liberty

He changed and became a burglar
In his fight for their liberty
Saved the caged slaves in misery
Clad in black he burgled the basement lab
At night he became an underground Sab
Freeing our prisoners from agony

So can you measure the distance for me
It's so dark here I can hardly see
I'm blinded by the light of law and our history

I'm still not close enough to see
Who is blessed and who is cursed
Rescuing a slave in a field and one in a laboratory
Who is blessed and who is cursed
Rescuing a slave in prison and one in a laboratory
So help me unravel the laws bitter-sweet mystery
To see the difference between these three
Harriet and Louise and renegade Ronnie Lee

Bull-at-a-Gate

The jaundiced Judge
Chanced upon a judgement
He had to give that was to decide
Whether the matador or picador or toreador
Should die or live as a tradition
Whether he could override
The bare fact it raised so much tax
With the ingrained abuse side-by-side
Should he aid its timely abolition

The Judge attacked it head-on
Asking the Counsel in a voice-weary tone
Borne of a sleepless long-lost night
Is the question no less than whether a bullfight
Is part of culture and a sport or just animal abuse
And so can never be right?
And anyway who can tell
Who has the right to sell
Another life or line or lie
About who has fallen on the racecourse
Who objects to eating a knackered horse
When fishing and shooting just rocks
Is no different to killing a fox
Or a stag or hanging a bull
On a production-line hook
Or research in a science book
From an experiment
Is it just another way
For an academic on a frolic
Using language that is hyperbolic
Finding a fun way to pay the rent?

The Judge waited for an answer to appear
A deep thinker he was known to be swift
Yet Counsel stayed silent then quite quietly said
'I figure on this one I'll take the Fifth.'

The Judge could see through his scheme
He said that is American legalese
Use English logic and law if you please
So the Counsel grabbed his gown
He figured it was time for prudence
He shot a quizzical look at the Judge
And said I'll exercise my right of silence

Calling out a Cow

Given she is a politician
Why object to repetition
Why object to being called fat
When most of us are just that
Or was it the fact it has a ring
Through her nose
Rather than holding a rose
So that was the thing

The drunken politician lingers too long
Using self-engendered power too much
Places the sober victim in his clutch
Balancing by a hand on her crutch
When she resists he calls her a cow
His sweaty palms and wrinkled brow
Spitting lies through an alcoholic mist
To deliver his halitosis Iscariot kiss

With his nicotine-stained breath
He brands every woman a cow
When she tries to resist his sweat
An ego-tipsy lawyer says 'she's a sow'
Matches his mouth with paltry power
Calling every pupil a diesel dyke cow
Even his huggery is close to buggery
While his sugary words smell sour

Why object to being called fat
When most of us are just that
Did the ring remind her of an auction
Seeing herself as someone's luncheon

Each of them sees the cowed cow
As something they can transform
Into their own rust-worn image
With a closet mental chloroform

Circle of death in Parliament Square

London Town on a sunny day
Maggie Smith's eyes are filled with rain
London Town on a rainy day
Maggie Smith's eyes are filled with pain

London Town on a sunny day
Dave Jones' eyes are filled with rain
London Town on a rainy day
Dave Jones' eyes are filled with pain

Daisy was starving and stranded
A pregnant stray without a home
Another mother abandoned
Until Maggie threw her a bone

Then they shared their luck and their life
Together through the windswept rain
Sharing their food while dodging strife
Sharing love and each other's pain

Then bitter snow shards bit and burned
Through her fur and their flimsy clothes
The temperature fell and turned
Bones to ice so they dozed and froze

Three bodies in Parliament Square
Three bodies without a heartbeat
Three bodies there yet no one cared
Three more statistics on the street

Politicians stepped by the heap
Of bodies long since forsaken
Lost and lonely in their last sleep
So deep they'd never awaken

The politicians looked away
Blind to the truth so plain to see
They stole the lonesome souls that day
Of those statistics of society

Though the tongue finds the gnawing tooth
Of sleepers frozen in the sleet
Yet they feign to forget the truth
Of faceless figures on our streets

Daisy and Maggie and Dave died
Just so much stale meat on the street
Daisy and Maggie and Dave died
Three more statistics on our streets

The question that remains for us
So we know where each of us stands
Are they just our society's pus?
And their fate is sand in our hands?

Closing Bristol Zoo

How the people cheered when they heard
Zimmerman's announcement that
'Bristol Zoo is closing down'
He had hardly uttered those very words
Before the grapevine celebrated the end
Of a hated place as an Animals' Alcatraz
No escape from the whooped razzamataz
Yet inmates had not committed a crime
Forced being born to live and serve their time
The joy exploded when his words were loaded
Zimmerman said it was a 'conservation charity'
It was only closing where it was located
It would soon be celebrated as a charity
Proving that as usual the goal will grind
When you see the goal that lurks behind
A facade that imprisons those
In caged cells that are closed
Without even looking prisoners will find
Zoos caught in a time-warp of closed minds
Zoos are run for us with a time that binds
With no key and no freedom from me and you
A pervasive panic on the face of the walleroo
Our disgrace drawn on a face of the wanderoo

Until a last breath guarantees a release by death
Proving what we knew all along to be true
In or out of a cage our world is a human zoo

Yet in Bristol Zoo animals are conserved
Now many Horfield Prisoners have reserved
Their next sentence there as they deserve
A sight for scarred eyes through barred stars

Cock Crows into a Cocked Hat

The cock crowed since he was born
Loved by the early morning callers
Paper-boys postmen and tip-toed priests
Plus last round party-loved rock 'n' ballers
Until the day the judge would not budge
When neighbours woke a crooked grudge
Content to condemn a cock's croak to cease

A neighbour hid in the 3 a.m. rain
Ready to hear the cock crow again
The list grew longer with her name
So the crowing cock could be stopped
A blade awaited a head being dropped
He was paddling and pecking in his tracks
He saw no light of law between the cracks

No one challenged the bully-boy neighbour
Strolling around the court as cock of the walk
No one delivered any defence for the cock
Who was not given time to baulk or talk
To make any sense in his own defence
His future was forged in his past tense
When sentenced to croak his last squawk

Destined to die by bias filling the empty dock
Words he never heard struck his stopped clock

The red-faced grumpy judge listened
Neighbours who had stood in the rain
As conspirators lined up to complain
While his ears twitched and glistened

As the cock croaked his last shout out
Smug buggers smirked with satisfaction
A law of Nuisance gave them traction
Glad to have the judge share their bias
Given his typical half-baked reaction
Yet he dwelt long on what he had done
He figured and felt he had done wrong
Troubled with his thoughts in the dark
His 3.a.m. feeling with unleashed reins
What if some nosy neighbour complains
About my rescued dog's incessant bark
Still troubled if it was already too late
Will some other curmudgeonly judge
With the stroke of a pen decide his fate
What can I do now to save that cock
Or has his doodle already been docked

Neighbours presented each petty point
Huddled as a cabal to silence the cock
Echoing each other's beef-upped joint
Another dead animal to eat and anoint
All ready and able to conspirc and shout
Lined up to find a cock to complain about
Branding her as a noisy countryside lout

Meanwhile the black rain lashed hard
A footloose cock strolled in the yard
A trumpet blew twice as he croaked thrice
Losing a throw of a dice with a marked card
His sound faded when a judgment was made
Followed by a funeral fugue tune softly played
While the neighbours knelt and silently prayed
While 'All Creatures Great and Small' played

The rolling wheels of law could not be stayed
Her blood dripped from the crucifixion blade
A lonesome cock strangled and swiftly slayed

Colston's Chains of Change

Colston paraded lies for 125 years
Neither eye washed a single tear
Without sight to see his wraith fear
Selling a coffle by checking shekels
Iron chains on bodies bound naked
Shot through with his putrid hatred

An executioner whose wounds never healed
Colston counted on his contaminated ideals
As those inside the bowels of his ships
Drowned or flayed alive by his whips
His vision seeing people as freight
A bent slaver who was never straight

No longer immune in 2020 on 7 June
Under a red sky lighting a purple moon
Leaving the links of Colston's remains
As the stale stench of a slaver's mange
A dead soul sank in the harbour sea
A dead statue for his musty memory

No force could ever hold you or me
Or anyone who is ever born to be free
But his biased profit from their misery
Dying to breathe Bristol air floating free
Their birthright of natural-born liberty
Chains of change from his prison destiny
Now is not the time to avoid the sting
Knowing a slave was legally a thing
As truth took flight on freedom's wing
Humans legally a quasi-animal 'thing'

Scarred bodies made the slavers sing
Gold a reward slaves' blood would bring

Even in a grave you cannot escape truth
Freedom's flag flew high by the Colston 4
In the splendour of Bristol Crown Court

Roots spread worldwide from our justice tree
A wise jury verdict that set the Colston 4 free
A pulse of justice beats time in the key '*Not Guilty*'

BLM means being free of a nemesis
ALM means being free as a genesis
People and animals used as an alibi
A distorted trope of our historic lies
In the fast-flowing river of never-ending ruth
Animals deserve the same verdict of raw truth
Animals' Lives Matter is one we know forsooth

Coulrophobia Blues

When I told the other birds
I was going to be a singer
How they all laughed at me
When I said I had a voice
That would make a bird jealous
Just you wait and see
The laughter grew louder
As I grew silent with lockjaw
They yelled 'we are seeking a sound'
So just tell us

When I told the grazing cows
I was going to be a poet
How they all laughed at me
When I said I had a way with a word
That had to be heard
Just you wait and see
The laughter grew louder
As I shrank on the blank page
No bells chimed as I had no sense
Of rhythm or rhyme

When I told them all
I was going to be a class clown
Then you too laughed at me
When I said my sadness
Was deeper than Garibaldi rust
Just you wait and see
I was boiled alive to satisfy
Your hungry biased eyes

Your laughter scalded me
As I burned in the Grimaldi dust

I was fooling while my unsprung tongue was silent
I remained being seen as a forever vacant savant
I told you I had no desire to die
Before I was even born
If I could I would bet you are not laughing now
For when you read this it will be
Only my lonely abattoir epitaph
Is all that you will know and see
So at last please let me be to R I P

Cuckoo in the Mirror

They come along as burglars
Then for no good reason
Without cause or provocation
Whatever the time or season
Rob the guileless bird of her song

Every day in trees and woods
Using force and strength at best
They steal all they want
Then dump each bird from their nest
Camouflaged by woods and trees

Killing is their trade
Trade is now so good
Suspended on the coop
Ever ready to swoop
Under a winged hood
Killing birds who cannot move
Fledgling birds are never safe
The burglars serve to prove
Action before she flies the coop
Calling and committing a coup
As a bird drops before she even grew
Nature's mirror detects the one who slew
Behind the guise of the quisling cuckoo
A serial killer lurks whose feelings flew
Nature's mirror reflects a reason for rue
The culprit's identity is drawn on a flue
A blurred image we recognise of me and you

Cull-me-to-You

The petals of the purple pansy
Used with a straight intention
Sends a scent with that intent
So nature needs no invention

Yes the flower smells sweetly
Except when what is false
Soon shifts to become true
Then the ones who choose
Which ones will be the ones to lose
Smell stronger than a Cull-me-to-You

Only a lonely victim whose lifeline fades
From being dim to a new place in Shittim
As the sure hot shot is certain to hit him
All caught in the marksman's cross-hair cull
Where more and more animals and flowers
Add up to the mathematics of our finest hour
It is high Noon as all we can possibly devour
Dying by our hands proves we are successful
Rotting bodies show no reason to be rueful

Each weak one we destroy is proof of what is true
Killing without kindness is our perfect Cull-me-to-You

Cycle of Life

She said with the voice of experience
That the children look after each animal
And finally kill them and eat them
That is the lesson they have learned about life
And how to manage their natural strife
Sometimes the answer is a kitchen knife
She said it was a vital lesson to learn
For in simple terms it is the cycle of life

While as any mother she meant well
It was strange she failed to tell
That what she was teaching them
Was opposite the words that fell
From her tongue to those so young
For the dead were always the dead
Because they were hamstrung
By the lack of a human tongue

Each creature they cared for
Could be killed and eaten
As their lives were fleeting
And their deaths the cost
They were bound to pay
Because in the cycle of life
Their palate guides the decision
It is as it is as it is the only way

To all her children
With no pause for breath
She was selling her ideal
Ignore what the animal feels

That was a natural prelude
As a reward for feeding them
Animals were their recycled food

Then the youngest child asked
'Mum you say it's good to treat our pet
As if it was splitting a hunk of wood
No reason to fret
Or for any regret
Yet that seems less like life we respect
And more like our own cycle of death?'

DNA of a Politician

Rees-Mogg asked Reg Presley
If he could join The Troggs
Reg was far too shrewd
He knew Mogg was no dude
When he backed *foie gras*
To satisfy his Somerset mates
Then backed the new GM
To kill any thoughts of ALM
Breeding animals resistant to disease
So farmers would gain higher profits
While animals would be caught off it
By breeding solely female chickens
So no male eggs were despatched
While share holders kept finger-licking
The gain from it did not escape old Mogg
Who was always something of a clever dog
When it came to making an unhealthy profit
Would hold and unfold a clenched fist
Figured it could be a new miracle-drug
A reverse kind of vivisection on a mind
Taking the tablet day after day in earnest
Might be a future once believed impossible
Einstein meets the bride of Frankenstein
To discover a new form of fire as Prometheus
Doomed to failure as nature's gaoler
Saw the definition of a politician as 'a liar'
Parliament a place where every face wore
A sphincter smile hiding their pants on fire
All doubt removed and resolved by a nudist
An experiment in belief to change an atheist
An experiment doomed to fail its purpose
An experiment to make a politician honest

Dog Eat Dog

Unlike the President of South Korea
Whose view is shared by one or two
Different from many of his citizens
Who treat dogs as their denizens
The President says he loves them
Only as a companion and a pet
Yet his view grates and resonates
Among those with lascivious lips
Staring at their empty plates
They say just get real
An animal cannot feel
A dog is only a dog
Moon Jae-in tries to pettifog
Instead of a pet we can get
A profit from a fast food death
Every dog has to face their fate
Being where they were born to be
In a wet market hanging straight
Then dead-eyed on a diner's plate

Farmers and restaurateurs are up in arms
Rejecting out of hand a President's palm
Trampling on their human rights
To eat whatever they want
A right to kill as a response

A few claim rights are wrong
Killing one to satisfy another
As if an animal is a sister or brother
While they hide their laughter after
Adding to the pile of burning logs

While a cage full of petrified dogs
Line up to be routinely dangled
Then and there simply strangled
All gurgling gut and minds mangled
Each stray simply skinned alive
Eyes fixed on a life now deprived

The farmers suggest a compromise
Letting the citizens eat dog meat
For only '20 years or so'
Then it can and will taper off
What a wonderful way to go
Yet given how humans behave
In 20 years dogs will be gorged
No less than they are today
The price they will still pay
Is a greasy rope in a rusty cage
A handy club and an early grave
Grasping hands reach in the trave
Each dog beaten black and blue
Will possess the same money value
Each dog lynched for their lunch
As a regular part of their daily trade
Once assessed as a bought body
Of another kind of whipped slave

Moon's intent was meant
To prove a dog was not sent
As a meal for every resident
But eating a dog or frog or hedgehog
Is the way it was and is all their days
Why otherwise were all the strays
Bound and gagged and sent their way

Otherwise they would not have been born
Much as women are meant for men's porn

All of it is where dogs were meant to be
No less natural than tuna in our sandwich
Rather than simply swimming in the sea

We Koreans see nature's gift in their birth
We alone assess what they are worth
These passing strangers on our earth
Their use for us is a verisimilitude
So morals and law cannot intrude
Ethics we can then nod and exclude
We can silently conspire and collude
Boiled or burnt or roasted or stewed
Dogs are born just to be our food
Failing to eat them would be almost rude
Your criticism of us Koreans is racist
For you English are all speciesists
Eating a cow and a lamb and a pig
Anything except one that is cute
Maybe not a horse or a guinea-pig
For us such reverse speciesism is infra dig

You have to understand we are real Korean
We are hardly going to become Pythagorean

Dolphins all at Sea

The Taiji dolphin drive hunt in Japan
Starts in September and ends in March
As a select band of chilling fishermen
Have a blood-lust that is always parched

When they spot a pod of dolphins
The boats move into a position
Where they plan on how to kill them
With no crime in mind or even a sin
For each victim is only a lonely dolphin

A steel pipe is lowered into the water
Shiny and sleek to begin the slaughter
The fishermen strike the pipe with mallets
Already they taste the flesh on their palate
As they poke and prod all around the pod
Scaring them all to become a herded clod
Towards the land to carry out their plan
The clamour disrupts the dolphins' sonar
Confounds their natural organic navigation
Turning them into a congregation of negation
Herding them from the sea towards the bay
To a sheltered cove for the pod's last day
The fishermen scramble to use their inscape
Spreading nets to block any means of escape

Sensing their date with destiny
The dolphins are agitated and aggravated
Because they are no longer free
So they leave them alone during the night
Until the next day for the fishermen's delight

They enter the bay in small boats to overlap
Closing every exit and route via every gap
Every boat closes in as each dolphin is captured
One at a time then their lifeline is fractured
When a metal shaft is driven into the cervical region
Of each lonesome confounded unsuspecting dolphin
The force of the shaft severs each dolphin's brainstem
So they thrash and twist and turn in the mayhem
A piston rod in her spine creates terror and pain
While each dolphin dies before their eyes
Drowning in a blood-lust sea of misery
As fishermen count the amount they will claim
When chained in a blood-guilt blood-red sea
Is mixed with the waves of pith-black rain
Yet even at midnight not pitched dark enough
For earmuffs to hide their dying-drenched pain

Now it is true that the Taiji killing method
Would be illegal as our slaughterhouse process
Nevertheless it is unwise to seek a false solace
For the Faroese indulge in slaughter in the water
In such a chilling killing fist as to satisfy any sadist
Year-on-year they hack the whales and dolphins
Finding their Grindadrap glory too hard to resist
When we fail to scrap their savage Grindadrap
An 'animal lovers' label is not dark enough to hide
As a pale substitute for self-serving disguised pride
Justice is never defeated by our contrived rip-tide

Duped By Descartes

Marathon mice raced against dementia
Another slick science trick on the public
Using a horse to find fault with the cart
Scientists set on duping us by Descartes
Experiment after experiment on our exhibits
No censure by a bunch of paid benchers
Deceived by a band of research activists
Funded by a scattered scholarship upstart
We are duped by scientists duped by Descartes

All the mice were strapped and trapped
Spent their life in a free running wheel
Then raced and raced every day and night
For us to discover how they might feel
By being denied sleep or even any rest
Wires clamped on each heaving chest
While caged and then routinely enraged
Shot by a hot electric shock-upon-shock
Repeated until every last mind explodes
Electricity skeins scream in their veins
All their fixed frazzled melting brains
Fry when our virus is set to overload
To decide who were the mice slobs
Or who was the elite marathon mob
Blood running cold for a science conceit
Blood running hot for the science deceit

Yet fat or fit did not alter their fate
All were obsolete as laboratory meat
Death their prize however spliced
Destiny rolled with our loaded dice

Data gained from death could not wait
Mice paid the price of being fat and unfit
Piercing pain sliced through their wired pit
Even ultra fit mice fell by that science dice
Hard-wired inside their dazed invaded brains
Kissed by electric lips straight from the mains

An experiment meant to prove dementia
Could be aided if a patient is fit
Yet if he is pleased to be obese
Alzheimer's arrow will hit a target
In time a mind implodes bit by bit
Mice racing four to six miles day and night
Each mouse became a lab bred guinea-pig
Dying from exercise or otherwise mere fright
As each scientist ticked a box
No one cared a Faustian fig
An exhibit mouse as a rung on his rig
A grant-aided death is one more gig
Just as a dancer skips off to a new jig
She moves on to her vivisection shindig

Yet a short-sighted scientist could see
Our problem is Brutus-style writ large
Is in us not our stars given the charge
When we choose to be obese with ease
Our experiments will never cease
We can vivisect an endless supply
Of substitute mice as our sacrifice
Mice can pay the price for our vice
We can continue to eat what we please
Each mouse locked up in our laboratory jailhouse
Each mouse becomes a stuffed-to-the-gill Diogenes

Scientists meet opponents with a lance
All that matters is they get more grants
To carry out more useless research
For knowledge as a pointless perch
Selling students another classic pup
To fill an idle academic curiosity cup
Inject a hundred tame sedentary mice
Then it is true all the active ones too
Selling us their pretentious cock-up
No time for truth while bodies pile up

A phoney devotion to every false notion
Gonzo science in a perpetual motion lash-up
Mice are our constant in-house sacrifice
A tame mouse as their endless leitmotiv
In turn leaves us as mercenary thieves
Parading lies while their lives line up
Speciesist thieves as silent as a Pilate pup

Even much better if we can choose a fat rat
For no one cares about our lab abuse of that
Then in time we can progress on to a fat cat

Marathon mice raced on injected dementia
Yet scientists keep well hid under their hat
A fact that will detract as a scientific stat
Gonzo scientists stay blind to self-censure
Many have dementia and most are too fat

We find the mice to deliberately make fat
Kill them for being obese how about that
Proves the thinnest part of each experiment
Yet we do not need to kill a single mouse

Yet we do not need our scientific jailhouse
Using a horse to find the fault with the cart
Seeking an answer that needs no transfer
We know in our heart and by the mirror
We practise self-deception as our expert art
Paying scientists to resurrect his pale ghost
Dupe each other then dupe us with Descartes

One mouse or a million mice
For us it really does not matter
Death is worth their sacrifice
As long as we can all get fatter
Their sleek scientific death kiss
Borne of lies as each exhibits dies
So many killed for so much fun
A number without a reason to shun
Three million mice killed in 2021
400 years later it is still rendered
As void as a silver-bribed Judas kiss
Then as now our Gonzo expert is lawless
Still reeks of self-serving Cartesian bliss

Even Dogs who cannot read love this Poem

I was just seven when I visited book heaven
After reading about Doris being a bad dog
Because it was so much fun it made my head
And heart run like an unleashed dog
And after the tears and laughter rather than a quick jog
I raced all the way home
Then when I saw my Mum I breathlessly begged
Her for a dog of my own

We rescued a 'rescue' dog who for me
Proved to be an ideal match
As he was a bit scruffy with a piratical black eye
I called him Patch
From the start we went everywhere together
As he became my best friend
When we went to the Library he even helped
To carry the books I'd lend
Often at the Library I would catch Patch
Cast a glance at me while I read
His eyes traced and tracked me as if he was echoing
The thoughts in my head

When I felt Patch was old enough I read to him
All of Doris's story
He listened intently to every word and seemed to
Enjoy it as much as me
Although I know he is not the same breed as me
He still has a canine need
To learn the facts and share the fun books
Will feed you and lead to
And as I have always thought a word

Is as potent as a deed
Last Saturday night feeling the time was right
I started to teach Patch to read.

Fit as a butcher's Dog

The stray mongrel chanced upon the butcher
Who saw him loiter near the shop's open door
But before he became a canine burglar
The friendly butcher threw a bone on the floor

The next day the mongrel visited the butcher
And loitered again with a dog-like intent
But he had no need to become a burglar
The kindly gent gave him an open consent

Then day after day the scruffy stray
Wandered into the butcher's shop
And day after day he had a hunk of meat
And on Sunday even got a pork chop

In no time the mongrel grew strong
And almost became a watchdog
So sleek with shiny teeth and so young
He looked as fit as a butcher's dog

Far from merely being a man's best friend
This was simply a twist of pure fate
As for no reason the man had a new end
He had a feeling that was less than straight

The customers made knowing comments
That pleased the butcher somewhat
For he knew exactly what was meant
By those who wanted what he had got

So seeing the shadow of the pound signs
Illuminated by the lightning lure of greed
He grabbed the mongrel as he whined
And balanced what he believed was a need

He took the mongrel out the back
Held him and gave him a whack
Then swiftly slit its tight throat
The unnamed mongrel dead in the dark
Barely had time for his last bark
As the butcher wiped his blood on his coat
No one asked about the dog
He was just one more butcher's stray
But was now another hunk of meat
The ghost of a stray on any street any day

The butcher had a honed sense of humour
So he hung a handwritten sign outside
Saying 'Toilet-trained Dog Wanted'
And waited with the numbers on his side

They wandered towards him each passing day
There was one after another passing stray
Until one who missed the one who met his end
She was searching for her lost long-time friend

She wondered where her mate had gone
But she had a sixth sense nervous inkling
Seeing the butcher was too friendly and all
When he kept kind of nervously winking

That all was not what it should be
Balanced on her mind as a weight

She figured she should turn back off
Something in his eyes made her hesitate

Her hunger would have to wait
Then the butcher turned his back
When she heard the telephone ring
She started to feel all a-quiver
Was she being sold down the river?
Was she another order on another sting?

She looked askance at his stance
His hands seemed to talk about her
He moved as if waiting for a chance
In that instance she glimpsed her future

Could she trust the butcher in leafy Bristol
Seeing what his wielding cleaver could bring
Knowing her life would not be improved
She ran as fast as her legs could move
She could see her future as clear as crystal
She decided to go when he grabbed a pistol
Though she could not read she saw the writing
The symbols said to her staying was not inviting
They reminded her of the squiggles on the I-Ching
Fear ran right through her making her heart ring
The feeling touched the instinct of her mainspring
Seeing his sign showed he was trained in Beijing

Food for Thought

Lizzie said to Maggie
As old friends often do
I've been thinking lately
About those nasty foreigners
Who are cruel through and through
I've been thinking lately
About animals and what
Those lousy foreigners do

Maggie nodded and smiled
The way people often do
Listening all the while to Lizzie
Never doubting what was true

You know those lousy foreigners
They will eat anything that moves
It does not matter what it is
They will eat claws and hooves

You know those lousy foreigners
They will eat the eyes of a fish
They will eat the soul of a sole
Straight from the dish if it is fresh

You know those lousy foreigners
They will eat a bat or even a rat
Make sure you keep your mog hidden
Because they will even eat your cat

You know those lousy foreigners
And it is not just your little mog

You have to watch them hawk-style
They will steal and then eat your dog

You know those lousy foreigners
There is something even worse
So keep your stable door closed
Because they will even eat your horse

Then Maggie said to Lizzie
Let's forget about the foreigners' habits
And the world those cannibals inhabit
What do you fancy to eat?

I've got something so sweet
It will be a real treat
I've got a chicken in the kitchen
And part of a heart of a cow
And a calf with neat sweet feet
That would be hard to beat
But if you don't fancy any of that
I promise your hunger will be slaked
I've got a huge hunk of steak
That will make your palate drool
As I always think as a rule
I imagine you'll agree with me
A meal is not a meal
Without lashings of gravy
On a plate piled high with meat

Lizzie licked her lips
And gently massaged her hips
Don't you agree? Maggie said
Seeing the body on the bed of bread

As her gaping mouth clamped upon
The juicy fresh dead fried head

From BLM to ALM Stem-by-Stem

The blonde bozo talks with a twisted tongue
Speaks racist sleaze in a sentence strung
With weasel words filed with sour wiles
He then brands children out of hand
Dumped and out-trumped as another bunch of
'Piccaninnies with watermelon smiles'

When slave trader Colston's statue crumbled
His warped heart and tarnished soul tumbled
Into the murky graveyard of the dark dock water
His rancid fame spelled in linked chains
With a face as infested as his remains
Of sad-eyed slaves he stole
And sold and slaughtered

Colston and Tory embraced fixed false faces
Serves just to remind us of slave traces
So we shout about and call out to condemn
From Uncle Tom to Jim Crow's Klan pride
While slaves and dogs were hung side-by-side
Springing from BLM to ALM stem-by-stem

Raise a fist to forget her and bend a strong knee
For a misplaced race demanding their place in history
Close the link between BLM and ALM
Make your mark with a single stinging stem
Now is the time and this is the place
To recognise lies etched in each frozen face
Of traders selling animals and black men
Whether wild or a child none were immune
As chains clanked beneath a white-hot moon

Lives held by a string from heart to hem
Balanced by worth in diamonds and a gem
Springing from BLM to ALM stem-by-stem
Freedom's flower blooms with every stem

From BLM to the same stem for ALM
It is time to rise and make some gentle mayhem
As a burning requiem for the torch of ALM

Wipe the sweat from your brow
We are all Stag-spanners now
Resist phoney Latin to amuse his jaundiced kin
And the lies sold in a greed-drive reef
Chlorinated chickens and cancer-drugged beef
Selling animals down the river in a slave skin

Raise a fist to forget her and bend a strong knee
For a righteous place in revolution and world history
Close the link between BLM and ALM
Make your mark with a single stinging stem
To sin by silence when we should protest
Makes cowards out of the best and all women

Furnace in June

Fear-filled faces pressed hard
Against the misty windows
Their screams split the sky
From midnight 'til noon
While the wild wind fanned flames
That trapped the unnamed who
Fried alive inside
The Furnace in June

The lady with dementia
Couldn't open the door
While her parrot roared 'fire!'
That cracked a mournful tune
No place to escape
As the flamed curtains draped they
Fried alive inside
The Furnace in June

The family huddled tight
Through their last long night
As blades of the blaze
Hit harder than a whale's harpoon
Choked back by black smoke
Goldfish drowned in a sea of fire they
Fried alive inside
The Furnace in June

The man in the wheelchair
With his mog on his lap
And his dog at his feet
Soon found none were immune

Their fur torched by flames
While he cried out their names they
Fried alive inside
The Furnace in June

Many people's tears
Washed blue-birds in their cage
Their wet feathers ashes and
Foam flowers formed a dune
Amidst the cindered embers
Inferno graves for those who
Fried alive inside
The Furnace in June

Politicians all talked
Clown councillors walked
Heard screaming rabbits on fire
Failing to read the runes
Closed eyes and closed minds
While people and pets died all
Fried alive inside
The Furnace in June

Mama, will they spurn us
Will this cauldron burn us?
Children cried in the furnace
Gerbils framed by flamed festoons
Mama, does anyone care?
When the answer was bare they
Fried alive inside
The Furnace in June

All the pale poseurs
Joined political pygmies

Spit their litany of lies
A parade of poltroons
If rough justice rings true
They will be the ones who are
Fried alive inside
The Furnace in June

No one counts those who died
Human and animal apartheid
Forgotten by phoneys as
Profits was their only boon
Numbers on the pyre
As bodies piled higher they
Fried alive inside
The Furnace in June

Pets and people in cold graves
When flames doused their cries
Burning arrows head to toe
Beneath a pale shadowed moon
Together they shivered
In the fierce fiery river they
Fried alive inside
The Furnace in June

Politicians played to forget
The people and their pets
Whose fixed fate was forged
By the blind buffoons
All bluster and bluff
Too many was not enough then
Fried alive inside
The Furnace in June

The mountain of lies
While bodies multiplied
Adding to the cladding
Of the fiery typhoon
More people and pets
Cracked a death choir then
Fried alive inside
A Furnace next June

Seventy two lost souls
Fought fate's fading spark
Noah's Ark in the dark
Set adrift and marooned
The justice-seat is sutured
Your past is their future to be
Fried alive inside
A Furnace next June

Goodbye Doctor Li

The WHO knew the Chinese
As eager as ever to please
Their case sprang from Xmas 2019
That was what made them keen

Before he could inspire us
Before he was sent to prison
Before he got the virus
Before he died for his vision

Doctor Li Wenliang was blessed with proof
The Chinese compliment was a total spoof
A virus spread from animal to a human
And then with each animal shoo-in
From a hot corpse with a tight throat
Animal to human to animal in Wuhan

Nothing could be denied
Though the Chinese tried
That their money is our market's wraith
So the price of fried rice is cut and dried

They heard the whistle-blower
Deliver a message that banged
Against the walls of the hospital
Too late to fill his repeated pang
When the virus that laid him low
Led to the death of Dr Li Wenliang

Grandma what is a Gorilla

There was a time not so long ago
I could have told you what I know
About our huge hairy foreign friends
Who happened to be happy in the jungle
Living by their own means and ends
Until they became victims of our fungus
When we used machines to make money
By destroying their trees and the honey
Then using all the timber and their land
To make even more money by our plans
So as we still beg and borrow and lift
We try to sell an idea our greed is a gift
A satire we learned from bitter-sweet Swift
Then sent in our own group of guerrillas
Now you ask me 'What is a gorilla?'
I am stumped to find an answer
Our theft of their home environment
Meant no less than our nature's cancer
All we offered was a bulldozer and a gun
We razed all their forests
Then destroyed their freedom
For what then was a gorilla
Cannot be disguised as vanilla
There are so very few left in our world
Their flag of freedom is forever unfurled
Except for a stereotypical view in our zoo
The Swift gift we can use without a trace
No guilt or remorse of any sort in its place
As we forget the feelings with no disgrace
Forget who we killed in our consumer race
For the last time we see their true base

I wish I could tell you something
That is much better than what I can
My quiet hope my dear grandson
Is for a change before you are a man
The gift we had we foolishly destroyed
The gift we see is an image of our void
The gift we give is wrapped cancroids

If you get a chance to see such a species
Grab it with both hands as he is on the list
For if you blink I fear he will disappear
As the last gorilla in the fading mist

Happy and Lucky walk into a Bar

Happy finds it hard to even keep still
He moves back and forth without will
He is acting as if he is drunk yet again
Pushing and shoving anyone in his path
Like yesterday looking for a fight again
With all who incurs his simmering wrath

Lucky straddles across the various bars
Ready to make any stranger see stars
One blow from her mighty right hand
Would send any man to the promised land
She climbs up the wall and grabs a shelf
She brings it down so pleased with herself

Happy and Lucky were geographically miles apart
Though each had a problem with an enlarged heart
It somehow sprung from them hanging around bars
When they should have been staring at jungle stars

Yet with home-longing they had much in common
They shared a growing sense of unleashed misery
Swinging through steel by holding onto the scaffold
Each was suffering from the echo effects of P-TSD
Then again it is the price you must be prepared to pay
When you are living on our terms until your dying day
You should not commit crime if you cannot do the time
Those are the rules that apply to mules and other fools
They apply to you too when you are caged in our zoo
It is no use for you to look so crestfallen and forlorn
You have no defence so there is no reason to mourn
Our bars are your prison for you can never be a citizen
Your first breath means death for your crime is being born

Heart to Heart

We are supposed to marvel at a miracle
Of a genetically modified pig manacled
Who becomes a blind scientific spectacle
As her body is poked pricked and probed
As her organs are prodded and daubed
Then her life becomes their obstacle
Finding a human heart as a receptacle
So the man who was saved
At least had a voice and a choice
So his decision was fair and free
Whilst the pig was only an exhibit
Whose life had no intrinsic value
Except for her use to you and me
For science to reach the pinnacle
Is all that matters for their miracle
Do they wonder what they would do
If no animals for experiments existed
Or it was illegal for scientists to persist
Would their routine minds stay vacant
With their vulture culture as complacent
Or be forced upon the pursuit of truth
Following a path of fairness and justice
Where we spared her life from just us
When they were forced to find means
By scouring all their alphabet genes
Equality would be unequivocal
Honest and fair and reciprocal
From our path towards injustice
Would not be defined by science
Pointless in part and useless as a whole
Selling a religious lie only we have a soul

Buying into an animal's use to us
But by a principle that is spiritual
Dignity is a code of a moral ritual
Borne of respect rather than habitual
So even Cartesian hearts were tactual
Now that would be a certain miracle

Here Comes 2024

Here Comes 2024
With our claw of the law
Hammering on your door
Nail all your lies to the court floor
We've got eyes on the prize and a mojo on the rise
Here Comes 2024

No one's above the Law
And no one is below
Regardless of their fault or flaw
Law shields the lowest of the low
Each one counts an equal amount
No one's measured as minimal
Whether you're a king or a common criminal
Unless you happen to be born an animal

No one's above the Law
When we balance the scales
It's always an even see-saw
Justice succeeds when all else fails
Each one counts an equal amount
No one's seen as subliminal
Whether innocent or guilt-ridden criminal
Unless you happen to be born an animal

No one's above the Law
Regardless of their claim or fame
Whether you're a prince or cat's-paw
Justice treats everyone the same
Each one counts an equal amount
No one's weighed or made marginal

If you're a first timer or seasoned criminal
Unless you happen to be born an animal
All are equal in law's sequel
Our moral code is seminal
The only sin worse than being a criminal
Is the birthmark curse of being an animal

Here Comes 2024
With our claw of the law
Hammering on your door
Nail all your lies to the court floor
We've got eyes on the prize and a mojo on the rise
Here Comes 2024

How Can a Man be another's Man's Dog

R v Somerset [1772]

James Somerset escaped from his owner
Captured by Charles Stewart on the run
As a hobo on the loose or a stray dog
Much as a slave hiding under a log
Ended up being tried in the High Court
A trial to decide his fate
Money was the prize for the slaver
Somerset stood to lose his liberty
In truth he stood to lose his life
It has no value if a man is never free

Counsel for the slaver said
Somerset is his 'property'
He owns him as he owns his house
As he owns his horse as part of his purse
The judge was prepared to deliver
The slave to be sold down the river
English law made a slave a '*thing*'
The same value as a caged canary
Or a bull with a rusty nose ring
Each his property no less than his life
Just as he owned his servant and wife

Lightning cracked across the sky courtroom
Counsel asked a question jamming legal cogs:
Upon what principle can it ever be an apologue
That a man can become a dog for another man?
In a sentence he declared all the law should ban

Lord Mansfield sucked in his judicial breath
Mulled over matters of law and life and death
Mused on ideas revolving in his confused head
Knowing his judgment would last beyond his time
Rebound long after his toll bell chimed
Wisely he reserved his judgment to be sure
Knowing he could unlock an injustice door
Mansfield figured now and then and forever
Law's free river could never be dammed
By a false claim in his juristic name
Lest law itself would be forever damned

So Mansfield decided once and for all
Fiat justitia, ruat coelum
The Latin phrase did not hide
All that Mansfield had to decide
The balance between freedom and slavery
Scales balancing English law against liberty
A truth that meant he would not hide
When he heard Magna Carta's 1215 credo call:
Let justice be done though the heavens may fall

The cutting question left him agog
Mansfield knew as anyone anywhere
A man could not be another man's dog
No less than a cat or hedgehog or tautog
Or a '*thing*' such as a bog or clog or log
As each struck within Mansfield's reach
His thoughts clawed through a legal fog
When he shot the bolt of his judgment
At once he meant slavery was almost spent:
Slavery is so odious that it must be construed strictly:

The air of England has long been
too pure for a slave,
and every man who breathes it becomes free.
Every man who comes into this island
is entitled to the protection of English law,
whatever oppression he may have heretofore suffered,
and whatever may be the colour of his skin...
Let the black be discharged.

Mansfield saw Somerset as someone
Who like him could be and see and feel
The judge first stood in Somerset's shoes
Then stepped inside every black man's shoes
Knowing the reason for his Jim Crow Blues
He knew a black man could never be a thing
He knew if he was wrong the law would lose
He knew Dido his black maid could not choose
He knew their future was much too loose to lose

Law still vibrates with a hollow counterfeit ring
Unlit and until and unless the jungle judge justice
Is satisfied when an animal is born and dies free
No less than a slave was seen to be an entity
With all that freedom can bring
As law is the currency of truth
As law is the currency of blood
We must declare in a jurisprudential flood
An animal is not a legal thing
An animal is entitled to breathe

The English air no less than the King
Their birth and blood is their mainspring
In 2022 a judge must have the sapience

To say today what sentience must bring
An American Judge Jenny Rivera
Said in the New York Court of Appeals
What no one but a judge could deny:
A gilded cage is still a cage
While that has taken until 2022
Law is not law that recoils
From fear to lance the boil
Saying what is and always was true
Now is not the time for us to shrink
An ocean notion of Pythagoras and Leonardo
Whose wisdom on thoughts of freedom
Is the quintessence of our kinship problem

When an animal breathes the air of England
It is too pure for the odious stench of slavery
The soul of the law is written with freedom
Intertwined with the sinews of solid liberty
In mind and heart to let the animal go free
Habeas Corpus should water the truth tree
Change happens at the speed of trust
Yet animals in law are based on human lust
Law is not law that chooses to use a word
Every judge in every court knows is absurd
Bending truth out of shape to suit our world
So nonsensical it has a counterfeit coin ring
An animal is not and never could be a thing

How to be a Rodeo Hero

How brave he is when he ropes a calf
Uses strength to bring her to the ground
Then stretches her neck nearly in half
Her breathing fear is the loneliest sound

How brave he is when he ropes a steer
When the hungry crowd roars and hollers
Using his force to overcome her fear
Then he makes a few more grubby dollars

How brave he is when he brings her down
Looking into her bulging pleading eyes
As she struggles and stays silently bound
He catches a glimpse of truth where she lies

The rodeo man with his big hat and no cattle
The rodeo man with a head full of empty rattle
The rodeo man who is always ready for battle
Sees his glass face in the dust
Recognises his mirrored lust
Knows too well she was his chattel
When used his twisting ropy prattle
To redeem his circle of tittle-tattle
He leaves her in a pool

For her fluids have no stopcock
Her grazed eyes glazed in shock
The rodeo rider hones his honesty
Placing his conscience in hock
Turns and twists with practised schlock
The rodeo man shows might is right

Using a creature strapped and capped
With no thought to her peril or plight
When the fun ends she is swiftly zapped

The faded blue jeans of eternal youth
Dangling cigarette hides an ominous truth
No saddle needed by the cowboy sooth
Sealing a dream for the forever uncouth

He stands as strong as a wind-blown dandelion
He brands her with a white-hot scalding slave iron
Holding her life in his hands on the ground
His boot heels held fast in the dust she lies on
His strength on her neck steals her breath
His buckle and knuckle invites her death

Later alone he looks at the night sky
He knows how he feels can never fly
Too many questions beg for an answer
He has run out of every reason to lie
Holding truth's secret as his heart's secret
Hidden except during his soul's dark night
He seeks to show how his might is right
He ought to know only right makes might

I Pity the Poseur Politician

I Pity the Poseur Politician
All their lives lined with lies
As they cast each false-hearted vote
So another animal dies
Their ears are deaf to truth and pain
When they fail to hear the last cries
Their ballot becomes a bullet
When another trapped badger dies

I Pity the Poseur Politician
Their tongues are tuned to lie
Finding their skewed kind of music
Blasting birds from a sour sky
They'll kill any creature that moves
A badger or fox or squirrel
Falsehoods float for the farmers' vote
If they're feral they're in peril

With an empty heart and a mind half-full
A vacant soul in a spirit so dull
What will be their next kill spins in their skull
They never count the cost of lives lost
Only the votes won in another cull

I Pity the Poseur Politician
For their eyes fail to see
Victims' blood spattered by the gun
As they face death without a plea
Without a reason to listen
As they find a tongue-tied scapegoat

They'll promise to revive hunting
So they gain one more tainted vote

An empty heart and a mind half-full
Matches their soul vacant and dull
Killing machines revolve in their skull
They never count the cost of lives lost
Only the votes won in another cull

The answer is stark like the dog that didn't bark
Capture those poseurs before they can bolt
Dispatch them with both barrels by the Pheasants' Revolt

I Swear I'll Kill It

You see my Bro and me
Well it gave us such a kick
To catch that fear-filled cat
Indulge in a bit of slapstick
Man it was such a crack a hoot
Catching that cute frit furry brute
Grabbing her guts to put in the boot
Then I tell you the best bit of all
Was when she could hardly crawl
When she was trying to escape
From my huge flailing shoes
Another kick and another bruise
I chased her until she was exhausted
She was scared and tired and weary
We laughed so hard we were teary
All the time our laughter chimed
So long and loud we couldn't wait
To share our fun with the crowd
Then at the end of the chase
She was trapped by my young child
Man I tell you Bro it was wild
When she was caught in our trap
I finished her off in seconds flat
By a repeated slap-upon-slap

A perfect ending of my chase
Smack and thwack and whack
Across her bloody unsmiling face
So we put it all out on social media
We wanted to share it with the world
We hurled our fun across the world

146

What we get up to in our party tricks
It was such a rush to get our kicks
Our new way to travel on Route 66
As the camera captured our laughter
Hell I tell you it was such a thrill
We laughed so it rocked the rafters
To see that manky Bengal cat
Lying helpless on the stained mat
While the camera continued to whirr
We laughed and laughed at her
My Bro and me seeing her misery
Our sour mockery of her heavy purr

A cat's value as one with no soul
Just like the cargo on *The Zong*
Yet they all knew it was wrong
Every game has a loss and a gain
Where a desert is due for the hurt
By Zouma and his cowardly Bro
Measured by a screeching cat's pain

A simple way to assuage
The violence of Zouma's rage
A Judge can put Zouma in a cage
Together with a starving lion
Whose lips are lickcd and licked
Zouma's pain is not worth a candle
In truth it ain't even worth the wick
As he disappears down the lion's throat
As a natural-born tasty drumstick

If you want to be a hero it is easily done
You just pick anyone vulnerable and weak

Then wreak your bullying violent streak
Find an animal that trusts you
You claim her as your pet
Kick her as hard as you can
To prove you are a man
Get a small frightened animal
An act as every abuser criminal
Do not dwell on your black history
Lest you recognise the cat's misery
In seeing you as a speciesist molester
Think about Colston traders as investors
Trading slaves' blood for gold always festers
Using prejudice to sell their English history
The Zoumas sold their racist speciesism
Of *The Zong* and *Somerset* and their ancestors

An epitaph Zouma could share on Zoom
Chasing a scared cat around the room
At 15 stone and six feet four tried to score
Swearing *'I'll kill it'* is my life in the raw
Zouma reckons we have to understand
'I swear I'll kill it' was what he planned
Just because he is a footballer and a man
Doing what he wants because he thinks he can

Calling his cat 'it' proves it is a 'thing'
Exactly the same as a slave was in law
With a Jim Crow and Uncle Tom ring
Raw prejudice never ends in a draw

In Alpaca land the executioner is King

There is a cloudy nirvana
Some distance across the stream
Where if you really listen
You can hear a seal silently scream

There is a clear nirvana
Whose secret is in the silver ring
That has a sight for wide eyes
Seeing the executioner is the King

There is a dark nirvana
Where truth has no store
As each one lines up
So the score is more and more

There is a faded nirvana
That has no meaning now
For every one that is alive
There is another dead cow

After the laughter
And the shifting sands
There is the sound
Of the pound as it clinks

Across a hidden heart
That was a mouth
Before their nerve ends
Were randomly cut
Then it went south
And now it is in
Someone else's mouth

In Good Company

Vistal Garg wired his cute barb
Sacking 900 workers over Zoom
He hardly had to leave the room
To make his point and shout about
How they were 'too damn slow'
Adding to his huge financial woe
They were a 'bunch of dumb dolphins'
Lest they missed his point Garg barked
'Dumb dolphins get caught in nets
Dumb dolphins get eaten by sharks'
Loyalty to those who made his fortune
So much money for so many years
Between milking their tears and fears
Garg's problem was he never understood
However much money you have made
It is never any good
To use a victim to make a victim
By a low blow limbo
From a dude well below the grade
Yet it is not hard to fathom
How Garg sells his hokum
You cannot buy wisdom
Or disguise a behemoth ego
Dolphins and people are not dumb
Though one who tries to treat one
For the other
As if they were much like him
Making each worker his victim
Shows we can ignore his gargantuan ego
Whose intellectual incline is pyrrhic
Words as wise as a Guns N' Roses lyric

As for rescuing a drowning Garg
You wonder if a dolphin could be bothered
With someone whose morals are smothered
In the scheme of things you might guess
They would rescue him nevertheless
Unlike Garg dolphins do not charge
Unlike Garg dolphins are quite smart
Unlike Garg dolphins are quite kind
They act according to a sound mind
Balanced by an open thumping heart
Dolphins do not see saving a human
As other than part of their altruistic art
If Garg had a modicum of their attributes
With time even he might end up being cute

Is the Polar Jury still Out

The snow white real teddy bear
Looked at the melting ice-cap
Then wondered to herself
Whether anyone anywhere even cares
She figured everywhere I look and see
As the blinding sun almost blinds me
Is our life vanishing along with my liberty

Now I have nowhere to live
I have nothing left to give
All I had last year has disappeared
I have no more companion bears
Heat destroyed the freezing air
Everywhere I look now is bare
I have neither food nor seaware

As victims of a human warfare
My present is now threadbare
My future dying as I am relying
On nature's invisible welfare
A chain recycling and supplying
One I still fail to understand
Why you are stealing my land

You confine me as your albatross
Yet you gain so little by my loss
A bent two-headed coin you toss
To render me to your underworld
To spout a shibboleth on my death
Words as hollow as my last breath
What is your gain as I lose my world

Now there is no snow white ice
But only a blinding solar sun
Shining through my translucent soul
A helter-skelter roller-coaster stun gun
I wonder if I am the last polar bear
Crushed by your runaway steamroller
As you stand and stare devoid of care

For all your hard acid rain talk
Where bears cannot win or walk
It is way beyond the time to ask
'Whether the jury is still out?'
For none of you are up to your task
The question shows you do not know
What it is about when you are the tout

The question will freeze upon your lips
The question is answered drip-by-drip
Instead of asking about a wildlife plight
Who wielded the knife causing us strife
Maybe we could ask the jury about
Why there is now no longer any doubt
Against you we will lose any contested bout

Asking any question about your jury
Forgives yourself and forgets our fury
It is a pointless pot-pourri of original sin
Our future is more than dire
Our whole world is on fire
You hide in the porch with a blowtorch
So your forever jury cannot now be out
Impossible to answer as they were never in

Jews Do Count

With or without an axe many claim
Jews are abused by those who choose
To rebuke them and malign them
Without any reason at all
Except it is just part of the system
That fails to control them
Since being banished by the English
In the 12th century by our pious bias

Yet abusing animals does not count
In any degree or calculated amount
A truth we all still have to surmount

Animals are prone to being prejudiced
For no reason except they are not human
They deserve to be treated with justice
Which is the same as most of us want too
Yet it seems strange that when there were
6 million people killed in Hitler's camps
Perhaps we would not want other creatures
Ritually abused when their cramped lives end
90 million animals are slaughtered each year
To satisfy the religious rites the law demands
Causing suffering animals even more suffering

The mathematics of our legal calculus
A trigonometry of prejudice by all of us
The unanswered question serves to perplex
Using algebraic custom to claim immunity
Visiting the consequences with impunity

Given prejudice on prejudice by faith and skin
Proving animals do not count in a legal region

So that some might well wish to question
The division between ethics and complexion
A law with self-created self-serving ideals
Might not balance how an animal feels
Stings the choice between abuse and suffering
Might be displaced when suffering is paramount
For it is proof that all who suffer also count

Law is our and the final religion
No one else can build a bridge on
Yet religion is only a religion
When truth is avoided as a smidgen
Then add to an animal's suffering
When denial should replace prayer
As death waits inside the gates of an abattoir
There remains the clincher and stinger
The duty owed to the living and the dead
Delivered when we heard what was said
By such a worthy Nobel Prize Winner
The redoubtable Isaac Bashevis Singer
A prescient Jew who knew what was true:

There is only one little step from killing animals
To creating gas chambers a la Hitler and
Concentration camps a la Stalin...all such deeds
Are done in the name of "social justice".
There will be no justice as long as a man will stand
with a knife or with a gun and destroy those who are
weaker than he is.

Jonah in Pamplona

Hemingway was a cruel fool
Who as a rule loved violence
As long as it affected someone else
Until one day he reached past the pelts
Then grabbed his shotgun
To clean his teeth and brains
One last time so nothing
But his raddled remains remained

Their hero and the hooded horse
Caught in the snare and trapped
Where misery meets morality
Forgotten as they are mapped
Confined in the crowd's memory

Jonah moved from Arizona to Pamplona
Besotted by the running in the corridor
Though he loved the gunning more
He would go anywhere
As long as he would find there
Some kind of death in the afternoon
A helpless defenceless animal's demise
Their date with fate never came too soon
As their agony always sparked his eyes alive

Hemingway was the classic abuser
Who regaled in the glory of the loser
Always being the first accuser
Of anyone who dared to criticise
The plain cruelty before his eyes
As the sight of a smoking gun

Made his cold blood start to run
Faster than the bull weighing a ton
Killing for him was freedom and fun
Killing was the rhythm of his mind
When death arrived he came alive
Except that is for the last time

Jumping Judge

The prosecution jumped up to claim
The animal was rived with pure guilt
Every point used to persuade proved
Her culpability was beyond the hilt
Every word they heard made them wilt
For they knew how the court was built
By bricks of bias and mortar of prejudice

Animals were asked about their defence
All they could do was shrug in silence
Jumped down quicker than they jumped up
Because they knew as with their kind
Justice never had any of them in mind
For them it was deaf gagged and blind
Always supping from a Socratic cup
No surprise they were sold a human pup

Then the jumped-up judge jumped up
As usual he was in his overflowing cups
His ruddy face blotched by too much port
Killing for fun was his favourite sport
Killing was his practice in and out of court
When he looked at the assembly of animals
He screamed 'We know all about your sort.'

Scratched the huge wart on his bulbous nose
As he sentenced the whole lot to be aborted
He went to jump down to jump up then curled
The animals realised at once that he repeated
Everywhere to everyone within our world
For in the past and present and the future
His world made their world a judicial suture

Just Like Joe Exotic

The Tiger King has a sordid ring
Joe Exotic pumped and preened
Across our distorted screen
Running a zoo for a bloated fee
Paid for by people like you and me
Yet when we see tense-eyed tigers
Cramped and crowded in cages
Manic strutting as sad stereotypes
Mange-ridden on shrunk stripes
Conservation by a phoney hype
Stress level rising through their rages
Tigers as tight as tinned sardines
Seeing the same scene-after-scene
We can feign and start to be startled
As if until then we did not even know
A glaring truth of all we gleaned

The trophy farmer's face contorted
When he steals new-born tiger cubs
Away from their perplexed mothers
Within days of their giving birth
Our betrayal as their purpose on earth
He ignores the low muffled cries
Of the cubs and of their mothers
As PTSD bites with no goodbyes
Two shattered hearts wither and die
As with those before and to be next
An endless chain links a vexed text
Serving to fill every vacant place
A hunter shoots into any scarred face
Under cold suns with smoking guns

A failed grace as our own silent sext
Blasted away by our double pretext
Between the darkness and the dusk
Hear and see the hollow howling husk
Of our tainted values writ large
Of surrendered lives without charge
Of 70 billion animals hour-on-hour
All fallen by our unleashed power
Slaughtered for their bodies and ours
Most bound together in factory farms
Where we harm them without alarm
Out of our sight we keep our meat
Far away from a natural vision-seat
Tiger cubs crying as stolen calves
Wrenched from a grieving mother
A matter of hours after being born
The cries of the mothers drowned
Their calves are swiftly taken down
We condemn the trophy hunters
As we chomp a juicy T-bone steak
Together with all the other punters
A life we decide is ours to make or break
A life we decide is ours to stake or take

Shoot wary birds escaping towards the stars
Then condemn those leaving dogs in hot cars
While farm animals are lifted then shifted
Across countries being hit by heat
Then onward to an arctic freeze
Our ice-cold hearts match bodies we seize
Our closed souls match closed cell gates
As corpses end on our cleaned dirty plates

Hear tantivy profits grow click-clack
Another racehorse killed on the track
A whip-crack spine and a broken back

Choosing to look the other way
Never linger over or even stay
Their dead bodies are true semiotics
Animal signs are our choice narcotics
Although we can try to deny
Signs that are an eternal proof
We know we are far from fireproof
For it is no manufactured spoof
We know with our hero Spartacus
Ideals flung under a passing omnibus
No voice to raise a rumpus or fuss
Alive or dead they are not one of us
Goodbye to the wisdom of Aurelius

No way to shore up the dam
Until the last animal alive
Is our final sacrificial lamb

An A to Z of the species we tethered
Each one serves us as a bellwether
Aware we are all in it together
When the abuse courses in our veins
Running through to remain osmotic
At once assume being routine despotic
A pale imitation of our hero Spartacus
A paler imitation of a marked Aurelius
Passing it off as naturally neo-neurotic
Each of us are voluntarily concussed
Masked emotion disguised and robotic

Who as true parasites are never symbiotic
In our unquestioned pain-drenched hearts
We know we are all just a perfect demotic
On a pixie-path to become Joe Exotic

Law and life and logic and Love

I know that while you were everything
In the realms of law you are just a 'thing'
Yet more than that crass legal sting
With a glance you made my heart dance
Then my soul sang with a wild zing

I know your life does not last long
I know until the end you were strong
All that was right with you
For me could never be wrong
For to me you will forever be
The lasting beauty of an unsung song

The law of life has its logic in place
One moment you are part of the race
Then you were gone as will-o'-the-wisp
My mind I find still tries to track and trace
The rare and raw beauty of your natural grace
Freedom I found in your ever-accepting face

These days you are all I ever think of
All it took was you to teach me about love
Each act as warm-hearted as a cupped dove
Inside my mind exploded in love's Molotov
As we listened to the soaring Rimsky-Korsakov
With you on my lap together we read Chekov
My hand dovetailed in your fading falling paw
Within the lasting grasp of love's locked glove

Law of your Jungle

Anyone with a hoof
Instead of a hand
Or no hand but a paw
Lives below your law

Whatever is your politicians bungle
In the serpentine law of our jungle
Skin in the game as a legal mongrel
We can brag with a meaningless saw
No one under the sun is above the law
We are willing to make an exception
When we consider the mass reception
For those whose voice is a hee-haw
Or whose grip is a fur mitt or a maw
Forever lost in our alienated land
Unable to grasp our withheld hand

Given your testament is fudge
Let me give you a slight nudge
As to whom I choose to dodge
When your hate lodges as a wodge
In the mind of your own kind
All we meet and always find
People who dress to impress as a judge

Your law is a veritable man-of-straw
For your vision is my blood in the raw
Selling us as tarnished dross by your law
A shiny slick sight is your glittering flaw
We both know would not fool a blind jackdaw

Let's all go to the Zoo

The people are all happy
The children are so glad
The wonderful thing so snappy
Is no one has any reason to be sad

We're all going to the zoo
How about you?

Zoos are such fine places
With all those seeking shiny faces
And nothing but education it traces
People trade glances as the tiger paces

We're all going to the zoo
How about you?

Yet for those with another vision
See through eyes something so true
From the inside there is a collision
By a group of our caged denizens
Serving time for no crime in our prison
A confused feeling has long since risen
With closed eyes she shared their view
For them our world is a kangaroo zoo

We're all leaving the zoo
How about you?
Eyeball-to-eyeball connected
Meeting the unspoken question
Silence followed the silence
No answer to the suggestion
Are you coming too?

Liberation Drummer's Blues

Another cat another dog
Another horse another frog
Another hedgehog pinned to the table
A tiger paces his prison cage
The lion roars with a circus rage
Defeats all the dreams of the childhood fable

The current makes the stray bitch yelp
But she has no friend and no help
She's seen as a clockwork robot machine
Strap the macaque on the steel bench
He's a living tool, a monkey-wrench
Hands steeped in morphine we'll never scrub clean

The butcher's cleaver blow-by-blow
Echoes the sexy chef's screen show
When the butcher becomes a housewife
So she can cut her cute conscience
To forget their sense and sentience
She can see the chicken as just a stuffed Steiff

The truth so blunt it twists and turns
As sharp as the housewife's knife
Though she knows in her soul
That one man's meat is another animal's life

We want a taster for the King
For the comfort their death will bring
Let's splice the dice so we'll kill all the mice
We'll still end up winning the game
Without a sense of guilt or shame
Seeking a scapegoat as one more sacrifice

Life Can Get Lonely

I had no choice in my form when being born
I did not choose to lose my life to every human
Given to you when I was only a floating embryo
Dealt a bad hand seeking the dreamer's sandman
Life often gets lonely facing death and death only
Given the choice we could have been the feast
Anything except being your rising obese yeast
Or even worse a trophy-hunted weary wildebeest
I like you would have chosen to be a criminal
Selling your skin in my scheme so you are minimal
Who among you would ever choose to be an animal

Your dinner-party morals sure disappear
When you take me down to drown me
In a cascade of my fear
Hidden by your fast flood
When my heart went thud
Then spared your conscience
Ignoring my death by silence
Less a crime or even a sin
A game you alone will win
With the rattle of a charity tin
To match your long-deaf ears
A spark as a lonely heart's spear
Bursting your gushed Niagara crocodile tears

Life is for the Dying

Being part of the killing
Of a creature you can feature
In stories of glory
About the chase and the face
Of the fox whose sly look
Shows Charlie has got a lot of pluck
Until we charge down with 40 hounds
To remove that grin from his smug mug
And as the first hound
Drags him down to the ground
And the second and third follow
And find they are joined by the other 37
That is our idea of heaven
With thundering hooves and claws
Which rip the fox from limb to limb
We hack off his head and tail
A sight that never fails to excite
Touches parts no other thrill will reach
Makes for a bullyrag jokey speech
About their blood-filled screech
As easy as squashing a ripe peach
We never care about their plight
Never haunts our Hunt Ball night

Our thrill splits the countryside
As our alliance is our science
For the bites show he has no fight
When he is outnumbered by 40 to one
Throwing him beneath our blunderbuss
So each conscience is swiftly concussed

Oh yes we showed that wily fox
We do not box and cox
We took him out and snuffed his shout
We are the boss
His life is no loss
At least to any of us
He is vermin and just our pus

Because we sure as hell showed the fox
When the teeth of 40 hounds locks
On your throat you have nowhere
On earth left to hide and run
Except towards our terrier man's gun
Except towards our man-made hell
Yet somewhere in the distance
There is an old school bell
That chimes to mark out the time
Of their sell as another kind of cell

Politicians mounted their steeds
To revive their country culture
Sharing making the fox a carrion
Politico prejudice their vulture clarion

Where animals are concerned
A lesson we have learned
Avoid the one whose tongue
Is heaped high with rust
One type you can trust
Less than a politician
Springing from the same stem
Is when there are two of them
Then they can double the means to evade

When their falsehood is ready-made
They are as honest as a sundial in the shade

We do not care for the drag
We do not care for the law
A fox or hare or a stag
We will smash the badger's jaw
We will snap and break their paw
We kill whoever loses our draw
We thrill seeing death in the raw

Links to the Lynx

The sleek beauty of the Eurasian lynx
We figure is rarer than a mixed mink
Though of course their coat still floats
On the back of a minx model turncoat
Yet around the year 700 we saw their pelt
Guided by our Cyclops profit-eye
We felt the umwelt would be our gelt
Mack-the-Knife style pearly teeth
We could use as a cute chess piece
Claws holding a book of our laws
Defining the lynx as a legal 'thing'
Now we are bringing the lynx back
Our environment improves by their use
Killing deer who destroy bark and leaves
Lynx strip bare with teeth that cleaves
Sharper than an inviting deer's throat
A lynx will deliver a model with a quote
To parade in a masquerade with her coat

An eco-system improves with a lynx
Besides we enjoy seeing them
Even when the countryside stinks
Then when there are too many
We can hunt them to death again
Enjoy our pinchpenny resolution
By a resort to our usual eco-solution
With empty minds when our land is full
Without looking we will find a reason
To abandon our new-found compassion
Replaced by our standard killer passion
For another commonplace 21st century cull

The beavers have been weavers
In the slow flowing River Otter
None had existed for the usual reason
Our kind of killing eco-season-treason
As they all had such shimmering fur
Plus insides of sweet tasty meat
Meant we could use them as totems
To meet and to greet and to eat
Until as usual there were none left
A bare countryside since the 16th century
Now we can let our rivers run until
We have more beavers than our fill
When once again it will be our time
To catch them in their prime
Indulge in our favourite mass-kill
No delay as carcasses decay in a land-fill

Beavers are nature's engineers
They build dams and fell trees
Reduce floods by the stream
Yet there are nature's side-effects
Their action can destroy the bees
Still that is only a small price
The real value of the beavers
Is mirrored by the value of a lynx
Compared to all an eco-rebel thinks
Yet the farmers remain concerned
The lynx will kill their lambs
Maybe the price against solid dams
The anglers rail against beavers
They kill the fish and even weevers
An outrageous act by a wild stranger
Causing an obvious devious danger

When the only ones with a right to kill fish
Are the anglers indulging in their death-wish

The links to the lynx
Is the corrosive chain
However it is rearranged
Never leads to a valid change
Hardly needs another question
That would befuddle a sphinx
When all we have to witness
We can already plainly see
Our natural face in self-disgrace
Is as nature's perpetual enemy

Check a century from now and see
How many are still living free
Or have become a mere memory
Squeezing their life with pilliwinks
A usual stance of homo sans sapience

Pound signs for pupils as our thanks
Gauged by a percentage at the banks
Their presence mirrors a natural jinx
For our life and death links to the lynx

Loose Use of Language

When the wise judge said
'Your words are a disguise'
He saw through our lies
We call it a 'trail hunt'
But our words are bent
To put you off our scent
To fool smart sabs
Get our grasping dabs
On the throat of Charlie
Before our hounds at the scene
Blocked rocks as our smokescreen
When we see a fox rest assured
We give the world our word
An 'accident' somehow happened
A coincidence he never escapes
The hole happened to be blocked
We see fear in her eyes is locked
The art of killing is our weathercock

The tune in our mind jukebox
Is to despatch every last fox
We know the 'trail' is a lie
As honest as blowing a whale
Harpooned from the ocean sky-high
Our hounds at his throat in the fight
A sweet delight sets our hearts alight
Our appetite will be fed
When every fox is dead
Nothing rocks like a dead fox
Believe me you except for two

We train hounds to break her neck and will
Their teeth ensures our game ends one to nil

As they rip her apart
We storm down the hill
Ripping her to shreds
Is better than any pill
However many we kill
We will have a void to fill
We will never quit until
Every last fox is stilled
We will scour the scorched earth
To find some other thing to kill
Then feign it is 'class warfare'
Because in love and war
Every action is deemed fair
To satisfy a hole in our soul
That remains empty until each day
We can grab her and have our way
Her last long helpless scream
Her hot nightmare is our dream
We need some sort of strife
Excite a light in our humdrum life

Hunting is our daily prayer
Why we kccp repeating our fanfare
Our critics indulge in 'class warfare'
As it is a line
We will not hide
We will be a pesticide
Dripping for their stillicide
Killing everything in our path
The wisdom of our wrath

Fox or hare or stag or anything at all
Steal their heart while they all fall
To satisfy destruction of wildlife
We can then live our lustful life
Our birthright gene is their genocide
We are self-serving natural-born killers
We will bring our own culls on
Until the last wild animal is gone
We will force their suicide in our stride
As warriors of a red-claw countryside
At the Ball we all make small talk
Laugh as a gurgling drain in the mud
Our excitement seeing their life-blood
We count how many lives were lost
We count how we won without cost
Drowned by our laughter as thereafter
We will boast how the fox was toast
When we loudly toast her death
With the unborn cub inside her
Sacrificed by fright right beside her
A glass of wine and a magnetic shrill
The fox as loncly as a whippoorwill
A toast as a boast for the next fox ghost
As we plan the thrill from our next kill

The trail hunt is the reason we thrive
Existing so a fox will never survive

Six Swan Songs

A Prickly Thorn in the Hotel

When Keith's wife died he ran the little B & B on his own in Cornwall. He was quietly proud of it as after service in the Marines he was keen to give his valued customers an excellent service.

He was a little angry when he visited my Chambers.

Old Keith asked me how he should draft a letter because he was really browned off with some posh jumped-up merchants and Bullingdon Boy-type bullies who irritated him to the core when they visited his Hotel in a leafy region of Falmouth for some Rag stunt or on a Stag weekend.

He showed me a letter from one such creep who asked Keith if it was 'O.K. if I bring the old mutt, Spike, along too as all the boys like a bit of fun with him. Though I know some down market hotels like yours don't like mutts?'

Keith was very upset and said he would 'give them a piece of my mind.' After a while I managed to calm him down and persuaded him to allow me to write it for him.

The letter from Keith said:

Dear Sir,

By all means bring Spike to us. We will be pleased to see him. We have a high regard for all dogs in this Hotel. Indeed I have never been woken in the middle of the night by a drunken dog that has lost his key and was intent on fighting the Head Chef or one who has puked up all over the new lounge carpet. We have never had any dog steal

179

our towels or go to sleep with a cigarette dangling from their frothy lips so we were forced to call the Fire Brigade where they almost set the place on fire. May I add that I have never had a dog that cheated me when it came to paying for his board or tried to rape the chambermaid or insult the very even-tempered and personable owner.

So please send Spike to us and we will give him a moist bone and a very warm welcome.

Yours insincerely,

N. Sweeney

PS. If Spike will vouch for your conduct then you can come too.

Job's Cat

Sam Spurns was walking through the park on the way to an important interview for a job she had coveted for a long time. It was not any old boring job, but a creative one that would allow her to be herself in approach and quality and style. The job would reflect her character as Spurns was a lady who brooked no dissent and took no prisoners.

As she was on her journey she suddenly heard a mewling cry from the bushes. She stopped in her tracks. She went into the bushes and saw, crouching in the corner, a tiny black and white whimpering wasted kitten.

She stroked the kitten. She picked her up and held her. She held her close to her chest. The kitten was shivering. The kitten stopped crying. The kitten started to quietly purr. As she stroked her the kitten's purr had its own gentle rhythm.

She looked at her watch. Time was tight and fleeting with swiftness as the interview appointment loomed large in her mind. In that instant she figured the two competing interests: does she just abandon the kitten to her future in the hope that someone else will rescue the creature? Does she place the kitten back in the bush and rush off to try and get the job of her dreams?

She was in swaying through ping-pong emotions as the proprioceptors battled through her heart and mind towards her centric soul.

Although it was only about 30 seconds the choice was clear and direct: does she forget about the kitten or forget about the job?

She decided that was no choice at all.

She went to the interview.

She took the kitten with her.

She explained to the interviewers what had happened on her journey and why she attended with the kitten.

The interviewers conducted the interview while the kitten gently and quietly slept inside her coat, close to her own beating heart.

At the end the interviewers told her that normally they saw every candidate, checked the references and had a second interview.

However by bringing the kitten to the interview which could have been to her detriment, she showed her true character. They offered her the job on the spot.

She accepted. She agreed to start the following week.

At the end when they asked her the question, 'Do you have any questions you'd like to ask us?'

She answered plaintively, 'Only one, can I bring the kitten to work? I don't know if she's microchipped or not and if so, will be able to be traced. Although I doubt it as who cares enough? I suspect as she's so frail and emaciated and thin, she was just dumped just discarded like the Christmas puppy with the ripped paper from the broken presents. If I can't get anyone else to take her, can she come with me?'

To her surprise, then as now, they said 'Yes.' She always figured that 'Don't ask, don't get', was the best approach. Now it proved to be the case.

Anyway she did exactly that and the kitten, named Ida B. after the great lady herself who was her silent mentor, became the mascot of the office. She was named and pictured on the 'paper' as a logo. She was a talking point for each new contract and project which both broke the ice and was a reflection on the company's principles.

Ida B. is based on a true case where the crème of the crème prevailed while Spurns and Ida B. Wells-Barnett were the cats who got the cream. The Interviewers told Sam they gave her the Job because she passed their personal test: "Be the person your cat thinks you are."

The Lawyer loved lager and Lime

A llama walked into the Queen's Retreat. He ordered a lager and lime.

The barman was somewhat surprised. He tried to engage him in a conversation.

I've not seen you in here before. Are you local?
No, I'm just here for a month or so.
I see. What do you do?
I'm a lawyer. I'm a consultant for that new factory across the road. I advise on the health and safety legislation.

The llama was not very interested in talking. He took his pint and went to a table in the corner. The llama took out a huge book and flicked through it. Periodically he read a passage and made notes on a yellow pad. The barman is intrigued and kept him in his vision. After about an hour he got up, closed his briefcase and left the pub. He waved to the barman who waved back. Day after day, week in and week out, the llama visited the pub and ordered a lager and lime.

Not many of our customers drink that. You seem to like it a lot?
I love it, son. Tell you the truth lager and lime is the juice of the gods. Before I started drinking it I was as bald as a snooker ball. Now look at me? I've got more hair than the average Yeti.
Well, I can't argue with that.

One day the llama visited the pub and told the barman he would be moving out of the area in a few days.

Why is that? He asked as they had become quite friendly. My contract will expire. I'll be moving to a new post.

Shortly after he left that day, the ringmaster of a visiting circus visited the pub.

Would you mind if I put up a few posters?
No, go right ahead.
I'll do anything to get a few more bums on seats.
Well, I have someone who might be useful to you.
Who? Tell me more. I'm all ears.
He told him about the llama and his habits.
The ringmaster listened intently. At the end he said, yes I would really like to meet him. From what you say I reckon our punters would love him. Would you do me a favour?
Yes, of course. What did you have in mind?
Here's my card. Would you give it to him next time you see him? Ask him to get in touch?
I'll be glad to do so.

The next day the llama visits the pub. He orders his lager and lime and sits at the table. The barman can hardly contain his excitement. He hands the ringmaster's card to the llama.

This is about a circus, he says and looks a little quizzical.
Yes. Great news. Just up your street. The ringmaster reckons he might have a job for you.
A circus?
Yes. Great isn't it?

Isn't that where all the main performers live in caravans?

That's right.

And the animals live in cages?

That's right.

And the animals are trained to do tricks for gawping people?

That's right.

And they are hit and kicked and whipped?

Only if they are aggressive like.

And they perform in a draughty tent?

That's right.

I see.

So what do you reckon? The ringmaster is dead keen to meet you.

I'm a bit confused.

Why? What shall I tell him when I see him again?

I'm still confused.

How? Can I help at all?

Yes. Why does a ringmaster of a circus want a consultant contract lawyer?

The hero and the fork-tongued Farmer

Leo Yeneews was a farmer who had a long and healthy respect for all the animals who had given him a good living all his life. Or at least that was his constant claim. He was so attached to them that on the odd occasion he even gave them names. That was handy when it came to the roll call in sorting out the next candidate for the one-way ticket to the slaughterhouse. Sometimes the animals had particular attributes that made Yeneews pleased or even proud of their prowess. He was especially taken with one of the unnamed animals because of the speed at which he raced around the field. He galloped across the grass yet he only had three legs. The front right one was missing. He was a favourite of Yeneews because he liked all pigs above other animals, but this one had wound itself into Yeneews affection because he so strove to overcome his apparent disability. Sometimes he just stood there looking over the 5-bar gate and stared admiringly at the three-legged pig. Sometimes he just gave the three-legged pig more food than the others or even fed him separately so his was the only snout in the trough.

Sometimes the fancy just took him and he allowed the three-legged pig to ramble into the kitchen where he would stroke him and tickle his soft head. The pig would stand still and look up at Yeneews as if he was enjoying the feeling of being treated like a family pet. On one memorable occasion a travelling salesman straight out of every pub anecdote happened to be passing by when he, Deke Rivers, was so taken with the three-legged pig that he pulled up, got out of his car and much like the farmer, stared at him. The farmer greeted Rivers and the two of

them stared in mutual appreciation at the antics of the
three-legged pig. As if he was performing for them, he
raced and over-balanced and stumbled and fell over, yet in
an instant rolled over and got up. Then he did the same
thing over and over again. It was as if the fact he was
missing a leg was a 'party trick' because he could barely
run fast for long without falling over in a heap.
Nevertheless, every time he fell, straightaway he got up
again and then raced until he fell again. All in all the
spectacle caused the farmer and the salesman to both gaze
in silent admiration and laugh hysterically in unison when
he kept falling over. After a short while the salesman
moved a bit closer to the farmer and engaged him in
conversation. Following a few pleasantries the conversation continued in a somewhat strange surprising way:

Deke Rivers: What a truly wonderful picture he is, look
at him.
Leo Yeneews: You're right there, son.
DR: He looks so happy. Is he always like that?
LY: He's as happy as pig in shite all day and all night, tell
you the truth. It's just the way he is, the way he's always
been.
DR: I'll bet you're proud of him aren't you?
LY: You're right there, son, rightly proud.
DR: He seems to be managing so well with his loss of a
limb, if you don't mind me saying so.
LY: No. No, I don't mind at all. After all he's special,
really special.
DR: In what way? What. Over the fact he's coping with
just three-legs?
LY: Oh yeah. That pig's an 'ero. I tell you.
DR: What do you mean?

LY: I tell you, he's an 'ero.

DR: Yes, I understand that, but what do you actually mean when you say 'he's a hero'?

LY: Well, everything he's done like son. Tell you the truth he saved my life.

DR: Are you serious? He saved your life?

LY: Yeah, and more than once, son, believe me.

DR: What saved your bacon?

LY: I know you won't believe it, but that's the first time I've heard that comment – today that is.

DR: Right, but what did he do? How did he save your life?

LY: Well I was driving me tractor when I suddenly felt unwell. My chest banged like a drum and I had a heart attack. I collapsed. The tractor was out of control and was heading straight for the farmhouse. If it hit the house, the speed it was going, it would have demolished the wall and might have killed the wife. Even worse, that would've damaged my tractor.

DR: So what did the pig do?

LY: I didn't know at the time, son, 'cos I was collapsed. But he jumped onto the tractor, changed the gear and pulled the brake on so it came to a juddering, shuddering halt.

DR: Wow!

LY: That pig, I tell you, he's an 'ero. He saved my wife, saved my life. He even watched by me until the ambulance came to take me to the hospital. He's an 'ero.

DR: I can barely believe it. A pig saving lives. It's remarkable.

LY: Oh, that's not all he's done.

DR: Really, he's done more?

LY: He saved my life twice, son.

DR: Tell me more. What did he do?

LY: Well, I was in the kitchen one day and I turned to go indoors to get my pipe. I turned too sharply and lost my balance. In order to steady myself I grabbed the handle of the chip pan. The whole thing exploded. The kitchen was on fire. I couldn't find my way back to get out.

DR: So what happened? How did you escape?

LY: I didn't.

DR: What do you mean, you didn't?

LY: That pig, I tell he's an 'ero. He rescued me. He hammered head on through the flames. I was on the floor. I couldn't breathe. Out cold. Well, not exactly cold. He caught me sleeve in his snout and dragged me out.

DR: Crikey. That's truly incredible. Obviously I you know, don't doubt your word, but I can hardly believe it. No wonder you describe the pig as a hero.

LY: Ah, that's not all.

DR: Surely there's no more to the story? What else could the creature do? He's rescued you twice when all is said and done.

LY: Yeah, but he even saved his brethren.

DR: His brethren? What is he, a part-time vicar?

LY: No, I mean the other animals, his brothers and sisters on the farm. We love the animals so much you see that's how we see them, describe them, even think of them. Really as part of the family, all of 'em.

DR: I see. So what else did he do?

LY: It's like this. I know some farmers don't mind the hunt on their land. I'm not one of them. I've always hated it because it's so goddam cruel, setting 40 hounds on a single fox to tear it to pieces. Believe me if you ever heard a fox scream in agony as they rip the animal apart, you'd be against it too. Farmer or no farmer, it don't matter. I hate those cowards, everything about them.

DR: Yes, I understand, but what did the pig do? How did he save the other animals from the hunters and all their hounds?

LY: Well, I'll be brief because I've got to round the herd up. Besides, it's quite a long-drawn out story. Anyway the hunters and the hounds, a whole marauding mob of them, came onto my land and terrorised the cows. They were all in calf too. Think how much they're worth. Think how much I'd stand to lose. They were all surrounded by the horses and the hounds. They were terrified. They ran way as fast as they could as if their fat arses were on fire.

DR: So how did the pig help you?

LY: He saw the lead huntsman and he got on top of the bales of straw and as he was riding by he jumped on him, knocked him clean off his horse and then proceeded to kick the living daylights out of him. All the horses and, for that matter, all the others were spooked by the jumping pig so they bolted out of my field and the huntsman, frightened for his life, ran as fast as he could, as fast as his legs would take him off of my land. I tell you this for nothing. I've never had any trouble since from the hunt again. They won't be in a hurry again to return. Not with my 'ero around.

DR: Well, I don't know what else to say. Frankly I'm simply astonished that you have got such a splendid creature. He's one in a million, if not more. No wonder you say he's a hero. How else could you describe him?

LY: That's true enough, son. I could never part with him.

DR: So he's not destined for the abattoir?

LY: Oh no, I couldn't bear to do that to him.

DR: As you have been so open in telling me about the pig's exploits, I hope you won't mind if I ask you something about him?

LY: No, not at all. You go ahead, son. Anything. Ask me anything you like about my favourite pig.

LY: Well that's obvious ain't it?

DR: You mean he was born that way?

LY: No

DR: He was trapped by the tractor when he rescued you?

LY: No.

DR: He was burned by the fire when he rescued you?

LY: No.

DR: The huntsman attacked him or this horse kicked him so hard he went lame? It had to be amputated?

LY: No

DR: If it was none of those things, how did he lose his leg?

LY: We ate it.

DR: To be honest I'm slightly taken aback. Isn't that, well, awfully cruel after all he's done for you? To leave him in that condition when he's saved your life twice. Isn't that truly cruel?

LY: No, that's what he's bred for. Don't forget I saved him from the slaughterhouse. So he's got to be very, very thankful to me for saving his life. As well as feeding him all this time.

DR: I see. That's one way of looking at it I suppose, but why didn't you put the poor creature out of his misery and just kill him? Then you could've eaten the complete pig? Wouldn't that be better?

LY: Oh no, I wouldn't dream of doing that. I couldn't do that and sleep at night. I'd have an uneasy conscience. That's the last thing I'd do even if I was desperate. No, not me. Don't forget he's part of our family.

DR: Why?

LY: Why? You ask me why?

DR: Yes, why?

LY: Because the pig's an 'ero.

DR: What difference does that make to you?

LY: You couldn't eat a pig like that all at once.

Jungle Judge Justice

Philomena Phucketyall [PP] was a ruddy-faced corpulent lawyer who became a middle-aged judge. Day after day she dealt with run-of-the-mill deadly dull cases involving shoplifting and speeding and the odd domestic dispute. The work load bored her to tears. She held on as she was soon due to get a fat pension that would allow her to live the life of Riley and luxury while idling her time away boasting about all her triumphs in the cases she had been involved in and her numerous animal trophies over the years.

Samantha Shytehawk [SS] was a ruddy-faced corpulent lawyer who became a middle-aged judge. Day after day she dealt with run-of-the-mill deadly dull cases involving shoplifting and speeding and the odd domestic dispute. The work load bored her to tears. She held on as she was soon due to get a fat pension that would allow her to live the life of Riley and luxury while idling her time away boasting about all her triumphs in the cases she had been involved in and her numerous animal trophies over the years.

PP and SS were firm friends and had been for almost forty years, at least on the surface.

From January every year PP planned her long holiday which was to get out of her 'comfort zone' with her Royal friends and acolytes and fellow parasites where she would blast birds from the sky, kill every manner of fish and execute every wild animal that passed her path. She always went with SS.

SS was a mirror-image of PP in fatness, lack of fitness and

especially finding salvation in killing any animal that was caught in their cross-hairs. If any animal was on the land or in a river or flying high in the sky, PP and SS would be openly glad to kill them for the pure pleasure and open satisfaction of seeing the animal die. They seemed to feel it was almost their duty to do so. As killing beavers and bees and birds and squirrels and every kind of feral creature they crossed was the first interlude to their introduction at home, their real thrill was going abroad and killing endangered animals.

Although they knew that the law had been changed so being trophy hunters was illegal, that did not bother or fuss them at all. After all they were the primary lawyers. They had such a vast network of connections including other legal eagles and politicians in their pocket. As a result they went on their usual animal trip to Africa intending to slaughter every animal that crossed their path. The bigger the better and the strongest was the best one of all to catch off-guard and trap and instantly kill.

They envied the obese American dentist, Bronkhorst, who voraciously slaughtered Cecil the prized African lion for no better reason than he could and had more money than morals. It was not too difficult as PP and SS had a guide and a powerful weapon that could demolish a house as if it had been hit by a hand grenade. So there was no danger to themselves, the endangered species were driven to an open pasture where they ate meat laced with drugs which rendered them drowsy. All the animals were then caught in their collective cross-fire. Any animal's pain counted for nothing against their pleasure. If on an odd occasion any pain was weighed their pleasure always tipped the scale.

Then PP took aim and blasted the huge beautiful harmless elephant into eternity.

Then SS took aim and shot the jungle king shaggy-haired lion so full of holes her blood squirted out in a waterfall that caused her to drown towards her death.

The swift demise of the elephant and the lion before their eyes was 100% satisfaction guaranteed just like the holiday brochure claimed. It was exactly what they had paid for, an experience and memory that would last a lifetime.

Back in England the Daily Criminal List was finalised and posted at Crook's Corner Crown Court. The first case was against PP who was charged with killing an elephant.

PP appeared before Judge SS. She pleaded 'Guilty'. Basil O'Doore [BO], the lawyer representing PP made the usual insincere submissions in mitigation. He told the judge all the good points, really most of which she was already aware, as they had been firm friends for so long.

SS nodded as sagely as a stuffed corgi in the back of a rusty Cortina with each word of the mitigation. Then BO sat down, more pleased than Punch at his natural eloquence, at least as he perceived it. All the roaming donkeys in the area struggled without four legs because of his loquacity in talking the hind legs off of most of them.

SS then went through the judicial motions and said, 'Although you have pleaded guilty to a serious offence, there are several points in your favour as your Counsel has so eloquently addressed in mitigation. However it must be marked with a sentence of imprisonment. But as you gave pleaded guilty, have many personal factors in your favour and have never been convicted before, I can suspend the sentence. You will serve a sentence of 2 years' imprisonment suspended for 12 months.'

It was all planned in advance behind the scenes in Chambers as the usual legal oil that lubricates the machinery of justice being a nod is better than a wink to a blind horse. Judge SS continued with her other cases. She then adjourned the court until the following day.

Unknown to all except the parties, SS was due to appear before Judge PP the next day. It was to be a repeat performance with their roles in reverse. It was agreed in advance as a routine example of the same legal back-scratching.

During the evening, as there was no work to do given the sentencing was already agreed on the nod, PP started to polish off the odd decanter of red wine. Generally she did not drink much at all because it made her temperament worse. Once she started drinking, she could never stop. That made her more morose than ever. Then she usually got to thinking about a 'life and what's it all about' scenario. It solved nothing except to add to her natural curmudgeonly disposition and suppressed depression. This night however was different. Something happened that could neither be foreseen nor imagined, yet it immediately changed PP then and there.

After drinking too much PP fell into an uneasy sleep in front of the flickering television screen. About three hours later she woke up and was troubled because her cat, Zogger Dredd, was not on her lap. He was there when she started drinking. He was always there. He clung to her welcome lap as if he was an appendage attached to her huge belly. PP called out his name again and again. There was no response. PP went upstairs. She looked in every cupboard and under the duvet and all his secret hiding places. Zogger was nowhere to be seen. His disappearance started to swiftly sober PP up. She went into the garden.

Outside the night was as welcome as a woman in a Taliban cabal. Suddenly the sky changed. The poetry of the night descended upon her garden. In that instant the indigo autumn sky released its rumbling rolling thunder and turned blacker than a chimney-sweep's brush. The sky cracked and flashed its message above her, shelling the roof and windows with hail and rain and lightning. The lightning cracked and lit the sky as the hard rain continued to fall. Somehow she knew that she and she alone was the cause of something the karma delivered by the rolling thunder. The poetic message was not lost on her.

Then out of nowhere Zogger was at her feet. She picked him up. He felt awkward and heavy. She carried him into the kitchen. She figured she would give him a rare midnight feast. She put him down. She filled up the bowl. As she did so she heard a strange mewling muted slightly screeching sigh which then ended in silence. She turned and was stopped in her tracks. Zogger was lying on his side in a pool of fresh spreading blood. He had a crossbow arrow running in and out of his body. She was transfixed by his outstretched body. He did not stir. He never stirred again.

She dug a hole. She buried her rescued cat beneath her feet. She had adopted him as a kitten. He was her only true friend in and out of court. She was no longer drunk. Instead she was out of her head witnessing the frozen pain in Zogger's eyes. Until then she had not realised that just two eyes could hold an ocean of tears, made worse as they were hers.

The next day SS appeared before Judge PP. She pleaded 'Guilty'.

SS had the same lawyer, BO, as PP had the previous day. He made similar points in mitigation. He nodded and smiled at the judge. Judge PP returned the nods and smiles with those of her own. It was as perfunctory as they had planned. At the end BO said, 'That's all I wish to say unless there is any other point I can help Your Honour with?'

'No,' said Judge PP. 'You have said all that could be said. No one could have said more.' Each of PP and SS and BO acted as if in a professional pantomime for the public who of course had no idea of the background of the defendants and their long term friendship. Equally no one had any idea about the planned expected sentence.

Then PP came to sentence SS. She looked at her and caught her eyes in a sharp focus. PP fixed on her for a while before she even spoke. Then her face changed. Something about the smugness of SS cut her to the quick. Staring at SS she saw an image and felt pangs of sadness about Zogger. She could not shake off the crossbow that pierced Zogger's heart. It now pierced hers too. PP suddenly underwent a metamorphosis in court. She sat in silence for some seconds. She changed and became hard-edged, frowning in maps across her troubled forehead. She then started to deliver her sentence:

'You have committed a serious offence. I am surprised by your Counsel's preposterous submissions, especially I should add, that all the while he did so you have been sitting there with a gormless smug self-satisfied smile on your hubristic face. Yet even now you seem not to understand the seriousness of killing endangered species. I would be failing in my public duty if I failed to send you to prison.' She hesitated and added, 'This is the second case of hunters killing endangered animals in this very court in two days.'

SS was riddled with a surprised confusion. She blurted out, 'Your Honour, I am confused. May I address you?'

'No,' said PP. 'Your Counsel has had the opportunity to do so. You do not seem to understand the seriousness of this case. As I said, let me repeat that this is the second such case in two days.'

PP hesitated so her words would hit home:

'You have the unadulterated audacity to come before this honourable court and claim your actions are a form of conservation as if you are serving endangered species when all you are doing is engaged in an endless chain of arrogant ego-driven violence against our fellow creatures. You arrogate to yourself and your cronies the right to decide which animals will live and which ones will die. Why? Yes, why? So you can massage your impostor driven ego to have an animal's head on your grubby blood-stained wall to impress other unimpressive people that you defend as your friends. Your audacity is surpassed by your mindless need for profit or greed when any animal that lives and breathes is unsafe as long as you and your kind have them in your perverted purblind sight. Your frozen heart-...'

SS blurted out, 'But...-'

'There are no buts.'

SS said, 'If...-'

'There are no ifs. You know you are repaying the nation of gorgeous creatures who are doing no harm with your industrial-scale abuse and torture. The animals are intent to live and graze in harmony with nature until people like you come along and pay an extortionate sum to kill them in cold blood. You are destroying their world and ours. Although in your case, it is not cold but hot blood, as you seem to gain such a thrill in taking an innocent animal's life. Why? And for what? Just so you can boast in your silly little golf club and at the fox hunters ball how you slaughtered an elephant or a lion or mass killing of endangered species. You are a despicable specimen of a supposed human being. It would serve you right if an animal turned on you and gobbled your heart up, although I doubt any animal would have good enough sight to find your non-existent heart.'

BO could hold his tongue no longer. He stood up and interrupted saying, 'But my Lord there is a precedent...'

'A precedent?'

'Yes, My Lord.'

'Are you serious? If you are you are quite wrong. Now sit down.'

BO sunk and slunk into his seat.

'Let me make it clear. There is no precedent. You might be referring to the pathetic precedent that was set yesterday where a trophy hunter was treated with undue leniency. That was quite a disgraceful sentence. Indeed that evil defendant should have gone straight to prison, where she belonged. If I had been the judge rest assured that is where she would be right now. However a much more important point is these horrible terrible holidays that these greedy people indulge in for their own riches makes me want to vomit. It also sticks in the craw of the public and society and the law. I will not be a party to such undue leniency. This crime is far too common. As I alluded to, there was another case only yesterday – as you state - but that makes your position worse not better. That is all the more reason your client must be subject to the letter of the law.'

BO stood up again and said, 'But My Lord, only yesterday when I ...'

'Please do not interrupt me again, unless you have something to say that is worth hearing. Instead let me tell you what I have in mind. I was thinking of a whole life sentence as after all you took the life of an innocent creature and let us be clear not just one. So many for so long you would need an abacus to count the lives of those you have slaughtered. You boasted and boasted in interviews about the sickening photographs with your fat ugly face and bulging beer belly and huge boot on the throat of a giraffe as if killing a harmless animal was some kind of laugh. Well it is time for you to get real. I will wipe the smile off of your smirking face. Indeed I would be failing in my public duty if I did not send you to prison today. The public are outraged by trophy hunters like you who somehow think you are above the law. Well let me tell you that what Thomas Fuller said in 1733 is still applicable today:

Be you never so high, the law is above you.

To upright citizens in our society, people like you slaughtering innocent animals for your perverted pleasure are a tinpot Hitler or a modern day Putin in another guise. If we allow people like you to be free you would end up killing anything and everything in sight. You trophy hunters are lawless and dangerous. I would be failing in my duty by suspending your sentence. With people such as you, with your proclivity, at large in our society, our community would soon become a jungle. Justice would have no meaning. So you will go to prison. I have reduced the sentence because you pleaded guilty. Although given the extent of the evidence you presented against yourself you actually had no choice, unlike all the animals you have slaughtered without cause or reason or provocation. You will have time to think about your past and present and future during the next decade. You will go to prison for 10 years. Take her down.'

SS's face was riddled red with anxiety and anguish yet she looked paler than a dead undertaker.

'I wish to add one point for the record. Rest assured that anyone who comes before me from now on will get a longer sentence. It will be a proper and proportionate sentence given the nature of this crime and the effect on the public and indeed the world. Now is the time to send a message to these criminals and to honour the memory of Zogger Dredd. A wonderful friend killed by another animal abuser.'

Her voice cracked as she got up and left the courtroom. In the corridor to her Chambers she stopped, stood and wiped her eyes.

The guard jangled his keys. He grabbed SS by her arm. Her face turned a ghostly pale as she was led down the steps to the jail where she would spend the next decade.

A cold cemetery silence engulfed the whole courtroom and the cells. Juggling with his keys while changing hands to grab SS he dropped the bunch which resounded as steel-on-steel. The silence was broken as the keys sudden fall sounded as sharp and alive as a targeted gunshot from a Colt 45.

PP was startled by the sound as if she expected to see an elephant drop down dead. As she left the courtroom she missed her step. She stumbled and tumbled and fell. She screamed in pain. She landed awkwardly against the Victorian iron railings. The force of her fall caused a gash to her face. Her legs folded under her. As she fell blood poured from her forehead and onto her face. She landed in a scrunched pile on the broken concrete at the bottom of the shaky stairs leading to her Chambers. A pool of blood spread from her mouth and head.

Hearing her scream, the guard rushed behind the court. Seeing the judge the guard dared not move her lest it caused more medical problems. Everyone scrambled into action. The paramedic called for an ambulance as he rushed through the courtroom. The next sound was an 'emergency' call to the cells below. Within moments they heard the siren sound of the ambulance, faint at first then getting louder as it got closer to the court.

By the time the ambulance arrived PP had not changed her position. She lay in a crumpled heap. The paramedic examined her. He looked at his colleague and gently, almost imperceptibly, nodded his head. His staring eyes told their own story. There was no need for words. There was no rush.

All her life PP found pleasure in causing pain and death to endangered animals. Now, sooner than she ever figured, she would join those who were her former playthings in her favourite pastime crime. She would join them forever in the animal netherworld.

The paramedic checked the time then ticked the box on his sheet. He then ticked the box below it. He handed the sheet to his colleague to countersign it. He signed it too, noting the time they had arrived. The two signatures confirmed that the patient, formerly an impatient irascible judge, was 'DOA'.

Dodo Justice

Law is the only moral system that can save animals from their lifetime perennial enemies. All the philosophical discussions in the world will not save animals for us and from us. They are entitled to live freely in a world they choose with or without us as they count in their own right. Well-meaning discussions about the consequences of a world without animals are ultimately just verbal smoke rings unless and until the ideas are enshrined in law. Justice is at the root of saving us from a world without animals. Why is it so hard for us to simply let them be? To live with whatever risk that involves according to the ultimate law, that of nature, given that ours has failed them? Why do we insist on a caveman existence in our legal treatment of animals in the 21ᵗ century?

What is the value of justice to animals? They cannot read or write or vote or engage in anything close to registering a protest, save for a final kick before being forced towards destiny's cell. Such a view though understandable is misguided. Justice is simply the quality of being just. Justice is performing the right action for the right reason at the right time. Justice is noble because it does not depend on what is lost or gained by those dispensing it, but the value to those receiving it. Justice is embodied in the Magna Carta so we can render what is due to a person and show the same spirit to an animal. Justice is an aspiration and sometimes even an attainment.

The future of animals depends upon our common law. In the end what is the difference between an attorney and an animal except for innumerable murmurings of each though as to which one makes the more melliloquent sound it is often difficult to discern.

An Advocate would examine the existing position and change it to benefit animals qua animals. An Animal Rights Act would concentrate on animals as members of our society with a value per se who are entitled to live on their terms rather than be circumscribed by ours.

Marooned rats leave the Ship

In the 18th century
There was shipwreck
In the Indian Ocean
Almost Christmas near Christmas Island
Where the sailors met a watery grave
And the black rats had another notion
So they swam to the island
In search of food and a home
And soon found both after risking
The briny foam
The killed the chicks for kicks
And pillaged the eggs of the seabirds
So the birds became food for the rats
And the birds were an endangered species
Where the cycle of life and death
Especially the reefs
Were in danger from the rats
Who were no less than
And almost as bad as human thieves
So now we can drop poison
From the sky
To catch the rats
And bleed them dry
As it is a drone
That is cheap and quick
And after all only kills
A pack of rats
While making sure
The chicks and eggs are preserved
So they can be served up as a pirate's breakfast
And as for any more shipwrecked sailors

Though perhaps like the eternal jailer
The rats on board will head
Full steam ahead for their bread
Back onto the infested Island again
While the rat pack politicos
Boast about their notion
Of killing two birds with one stone
By never leaving the wildlife alone
With their mission in motion
First is how to make the sky die
Second is to destroy the ocean

Meet Me beneath the Magic of our Moon

I never realised that just two eyes
Could hold so many tears
Until I lost you I never knew blue-on-blue
Would force me to reveal my red raw fears

My head and your heart are two worlds apart
With no one I can trust
Every night I'm awake with this ache I can't fake
It's just that I'm lost without your stardust

Without you my feline friend
My world has come to an end
My spirit has turned to rust
My soul seeks the spark of your stardust
Without you the midnight sky has no stars
My mind is chained inside locked lovelorn bars
Without you the night has no moon
My heartstrings are all out of tune
Yet we can read the rhythm of our natural rune
If you meet me beneath the magic of our moon

It is not too late for us to fight fate
See you in a new world
We could be free from the prison of destiny
To find all we lost without your stardust

M57

In 2021 a cop in Italy
Intent on arresting a felon
Was quickly cuffed by M57
So he arrested M57 for an assault
The cop put him in a barred vault
Then placed him in gaol without bail
A judge with wisdom borne of experience
Realised nameless M57 was not aggressive
Except in gaol rather than the welcome
Of his friends and the forest and freedom
Dismissing a lame lawyer's whining holler
For a few pounds bail and a forensic collar
They could track his freewheeling movements
For what was obvious to the judge
Should have been obvious to a cop
M57 should not be confined in a cell
He needed and wanted to be free
No less than chains holding you or me
Especially given he was arrested
Simply for acting in self-defence
No doubt we would all do the same
So M57 could hardly be blamed
As a matter of fact his single act
Was one both simple and true
While M57 did resist arrest
His predicament was manifest
No different if it was me or you
How you would feel clad in steel
Resisting a cop putting on handcuffs
He hit the cop once to make him stop
M57 acted as any grizzly bear would do

Mouse-proof Science

With a feeling colder than Arctic ice
The white-coated scientist loaded the dice
Grabbed another batch to splice
Inject them with their nasty spice
So many they appear as grains of rice
Lined up as another sacrifice
To find a cure for very kind of lice
And every kind of human vice
Complete each exercise at least twice
And then repeat it in a thrice
Blind and deafen and their limbs ready to slice
By taking the scientific community advice
Always calculated and opaque and concise
Strap them in a metal device
Whatever you do avoid being over-nice

After all the doped-up hordes
Are only a bunch of miniature rats
Or being even more precise
Paying the price of being mice
On their one-way journey
As they travel to the land of endless Nod
While we are vivisectionists playing God
So we can send them to a science paradise

It is easy to say about a chimpanzee
That they are 98.8% the same as you and me
You could even say the same about a donkey
But we can do whatever we want to mice
Because the public are unlike Herman
Who eulogised a mouse who was his friend

While they see mice as a form of vermin
Mice are not worth the candle
They are not even worth the wick
So they get their kicks
Failing to kick against the pricks

My Forever Friend

Though you're gone from me never to return
The ashes of my heart burns and burns
Something you said with a look is the best lesson I
learned
We have no time to lose or lie
In living and loving before we die

It's hard to know some things are meant to be
It was me for you and you for me
So I'm still mesmerised by your gypsy mystery
Though you tried so hard to explain
We two will never pass this way again
When the road was rough
When the times were tough
When I never had enough
You were everything and more to me
Sanctuary
Since your demise there's no time for dry eyes
How it was and is and always will be just you for me
Sanctuary
Only one had the skeleton key to reach the riff of my raff
You with your untamed beauty and wild country cat
laugh

To hide a while behind the sad sweet smile
Knowing sadness is always in style
You unlocked the secret of every unsung song
Holding each moment way too long
For now alone together we belong
Sanctuary

We stood face to face to meet our last task
Sanctuary
There was no reason for any mask
Sanctuary

You were there at the start I was there at the end
My lodestar guide at every wend
My North Star and forever friend
Farewell my faithful feline friend
Last goodbyes under Somerset skies

No Longer Born To Run

She is too old to be of much use now
A champion to one without a pantheon
Age has frittered her fitness somehow
She once was a fine athlete
Now she awaits her lonely fate
No visitors no cups no cards
From a Home to a lonely graveyard

Her legs are weak
Her gait is unsteady
Her speed has long since gone
She is getting frailer by the day
Even her sight has faded away
No one cares about her now
As pointless as a milk-less cow

Lifelines etched on her face
Nothing is rewarded now
All the money has faded
All the memories are erased

You do not need to be a bloodhound
To see the bounce between any senior
As each is unwanted and stands alone
Abandoned and as real as a dead clone
Seeking a chop and home of their own
A pale perfection of our confection
Her day in the sun and her race is run
Mirrored on a moneyed merry-go-round
Stopped short in her tracks by a stun gun
A vernier value of any unwanted greyhound

No reason for Rue for a 'Roo

Such a stunning sight on shifting sand
The kangaroos have roamed this land
For 20 million years as nature planned
Our Coat of Arms symbol since 1773
Depicts the kangaroo in all its majesty
No reason nor rhyme for a ruse
Australia is a country fit for animals
A true image of how we view kangaroos
Australia's image as a sanctuary for 'roos

Yet now is not time for phoney pith
Time to dispense with history's myth
For who were once valued as iconic
Now smell with a stale death's tonic
As a hop skip and jump before being dumped
Beneath the bullets as a sawn-off is pumped
A mountain of bodies bulge as a badge for their ruin
From politicians failing to follow the Declaration of Yuin
The Australian principles move to echo the Saturnalia
So the Joey learned as far as the government is concerned
From their youth for them ruth has no truth in their history
A fake Coat of Arms as an emblem of their endless misery

Our Spring will make a soulless heart sing
By a shotgun kiss for a bird on the wing
So be sure pay a visit to old Oz because
After escaping from the crowded beach
You will find a cove beyond the reach
Of most creatures except those whose
Low siren call is a death-knell screech
When their bounce and running just ends

The ones with no purpose and no friends
A natural medicine to cure every disease
Doing whatever you want when you please
Bring the 'roo and Joey down to their knees
No cause for any taboo
No question from anyone
No doubt about what is true
No reason for rue for a 'roo
Remember killing a kangaroo is indeed a good deed
Remember killing a kangaroo is the right thing to do

In black summer it is better than a drummer
A-pounding sound of a tow-bar on a brain
As a 'roo dies to the rhythm of their pain
Out of the busy city an itchy bug bit me
A frightened Joey in a mother's furry pouch
Lazy looking and as purposeless as a slouch
A no gloved specimen of a pugilist crew
You can find the ocean wave blue-on-blue
You can swim and seek a shark or two
You can even find the sun and some sex
Then when you decide what to do next
There is simply nothing you can substitute
For finding someone both helpless and mute
Waiting for someone to batter her or to shoot
Cutting down a creature in mid-motion is cute
No reason for rue for a 'roo
Remember killing a kangaroo is indeed a good deed
Remember killing a kangaroo is the right thing to do

Autumn it is the perfect camouflage season
Wander into the bush with a single reason
Seeing someone lurking there idling their time

With a licence to kill catch them in their prime
All you need is a warped mind and a weapon
No cause for a protest or some kind of sermon
You can be a jackboot Klansman with a jackknife
Then use your force and strength to take their life
That is the way it was always meant to be
A death fast and loose is their only destiny
They all fall heavy when their time has come
A faded scream as their body becomes numb
When the shooter's eyes light with excitement
An animal abuser without fault in his judgement
Thanking the fire the floods and the government
No reason for rue for a 'roo
Remember killing a kangaroo is indeed a good deed
Remember killing a kangaroo is the right thing to do

In the winter you can choose to splinter
The 'roos being born to be abused and used
As a pair of gloves or de luxe running shoes
While old-time Oz sprung from criminals
We can forge our future we know is liminal
By killing the lowest of the low the animals
Especially as each startled fur-lined hopper
In turn turns and becomes a scared cropper
You might take down two with a one bullet
A lucky strike to produce an orphan pauper
We decide which of the pests we will abort
'Roos captured in our own kangaroo court
Caught in our cross-fire devoid of a Voice
In law and life killing them is our choice
Willing silent victims of pure prejudice
No reason for rue for a 'roo

Remember killing a kangaroo is indeed a good deed
Remember killing a kangaroo is the right thing to do

Our criminal past is the one that was
Our present is a killing fun just because
Our future is formed and fixed on nature
Our rivers gently flow and time stands still
Our Joey breathes so she's yours to kill
Our history and inheritance is written in sand
Our Kangaroo Code kills them as we planned

Our sanctioned slaughter has been lodged
All the kangaroos have to do to live is dodge
The bullets and knives that steal their lives
As the mob parading as our government
Attack the mobs so their time is all spent
When the young-at-foot are chased off the road
Forced to find a new abode of a land-fill coffin
Killed by us kingpins for their body and skins
Our national treasure now used for our pleasure
A hunter and a punter wins by the Kangaroo Code
Killing without conscience is our marketing mode
Caged by fences and fires and floods
While they spill and lose their lifeblood
A one-way love-hate story of greed and glory
Our perpetual slaughter of speciesist prejudice
Written in water and borne of our human bias
Each Joey and wallaroo have no legal value
A kangaroo killing is our political hullabaloo
So when we ask the perennial Australian question
Do the kangaroos ever have 'A Fair Go'?
We already know the repeating resounding answer:
No No No!

On the Rack

The suffragette burned with a passion
That was outweighed by compassion
Without a care for the ideas in fashion
She figured that vivisection was false
Learned from an 'English Hungers' waltz
The sold science was total schmalz
So a bunch of Stag-spanner sabs
Burgled the locked experimental lab
Grabbed the scientists who dished
Death's rewards to their exhibits
Representing their mantra wish
As a daily chant to gain a grant
While the exhibits were unable to move
Used to prove the academic conundrum:
Whether rape is sexual or borne of power
Everyone knew the cue was pure bunkum

Sabs used their power at the midnight hour
They grabbed and placed in the same space
Science had reserved for the two chimps
By the state-aided academic pair of pimps
Their pale bodies shrunk into a deadly limp
Then the scientists performed the same task
When the pain and pressure pierced their minds
They did not have to look too far to find
The answer to their question about power or sex
As the force of the sabs was set to destroy them
Proved the practice was no less than a human hex

They wondered as they felt the fire
Though they tried to hide their pain

Using a mental state on their loss and gain
Both died wondering whether with Kant:
If we survive could we use our daily chant
To trail our holy grail to gain one last grant
Then subject truth to a scientific transplant?

One and two and Zero

Now in the winter of some frost-ridden scene
Turned upside down so truth can hardly be seen
So different from what you might have been
Yet your invisible thread is still evergreen

While I learned from you my feline friends' collection
Is simple but complex with a shape that is convex
Without a need for magic or a moon that shone
With nothing to be lost and everything to be won

Only clear-eyed beauty goes on and on
This side of the grave your vision saved me
From the spectre of missing and musing
Always letting go of my losing and proving
It is you who braved my misery and forgave me

The eternal equation between me with you
Show the mathematics of life is untrue
Heart losing heart equals a constant rue
Always adds up to one and two and zero
When I am caught now without my hero
My natural stance against it is to be a pierrot

One Man's Grouse/One Man's Gross

One man thinks it is grand to shoot grouse
Yet one says such action makes him a louse
He says you do not understand the countryside
He goes so far as to say they are all one-eyed
Though whether he means the birds or sabs
Is not clear as one-eyed
Might be the grouse who died
It could be the jack and queens
What he means is the dead-eyed
Face of the blue-bird
As the hunters in a herd
Blast them from the skies
While the one-eyed jacks stare away from justice
In a way that equally must see the pus that this
Wounded bird exudes as the hunters drink
To the health of those that they bagged
As their blood ran hot and truth was gagged
Sharing thoughts of how many they killed
Being so thrilled by the blood they spilled
While the second man might even be right
Given that the one-eyed could be
The staring face of Janus
Known to be false-eyed
As having been phoney tinker
Talking from his straining sphincter
Yet it could be one man is on song
For even one who is always wrong
Can by chance be right
Regardless of the peril
So the one with a mind defiled
Would try to justify rape of the wild

Sometimes much as a biased man
Is forced to see a harsh truth
For even a purblind hunter
Used to babble purely feral
Could stumble over a squirrel

Our Holocaust Sacrifice

The inside of a circle
That passes through a hole
Emits the same emptiness
That passes through each soul
Denying without buying a truth
Becomes the primary reason
Of our each nature's season
Is met by our nature's treason
Of those whose purpose is to serve
Killing them to satisfy a craving
As for us no life of theirs
Can ever be worth saving
Each one born for our use
Though we know it is no excuse
While we tightly tie the loose noose
To avoid being discovered or defrocked
Or excommunicated for having rocked
A foundation stone of our history holocaust
Before its current claim had an unpaid cost
Where millions of animals were slaughtered
Mere merchandise in our religious sacrifice
We can forget the timely commercial gloss
Knowing silence is our only riposte
For the 8 million horses purposely lost
Becoming a pile of our war's compost
Abandoned and shot and starved in permafrost
Without feeling for our gift-free Pentecost
Who we then casually tossed
Into the bullet-spun cauldron
Like the origin of killing on our altar
With no reason for us to halt or falter

In using a 'whole burnt' animal sacrifice
Their death's no less than their life's price
A religious practice we have yet to exhaust
As we continue killing the unwilling
It is a doddle using them as cannon fodder
In our World War Animal holocaust

Paulo the Pussyfooter

In the blackness of night
He was right out of sight
Paulo scaled the drainpipe
He was greeted by a scene
Reflecting a moon in his happy face
There on the line was the frilly lace
Scrambled across the line for an ace

Dancing as a squirrel not a cat
He brought it down on the grass
Held the lace between his teeth
The bra dangled as a saxophone
He swiftly snatched it fancy that
As if he was a dog with a bone
Balancing as a high-wire cat
Paulo scarpered to safety racing home

The next day he wandered afar
Peering into the darkest garden
Past the priest's early morn sermon
Before the lady's pants were missed
Hidden by the fast fading grey mist
Before her last secret partner's kiss
Paulo brought her the pink lacy pants
His owner was somewhat taken aback
She looked at Paulo somewhat askance
'You're a badass cat that's for sure'
Half-smiled for he touched her core

Until that is the next dark night
When Paulo lit out at midnight

As usual he was up to no good
Prowling in the neighbourhood
Paulo chanced upon a hip group
Listening entranced to a music loop
Followed by an odd holler and a hoop
As they smoked Paulo quietly snooped
Hiding in the shadows ready to swoop

Laying out flat as the music played
Paulo had no reason to be afraid
Amused he caught a pipe in his paw
Juggled and hooked the tobacco too
Which the group covertly grew
Paulo's act was perhaps a bit rash
As he had grabbed their secret stash
Pure punk skunk was high value cash

Yet no longer as a passing stranger
Pussyfoot Paulo relished the danger
Paulo never stayed for very long
Before the strain of the last song
Paulo was already up and gone
He swiftly returned to his mistress
Getting back to where he belonged
Flying fast with the wind
In a night-time heady pong
His head was spinning with a winning song
Clenched teeth clasped a classic brass bong

His prowess was put to the test
Paulo saw that Patsy had pressed
The black bra close to her chest

Smiled and changed with a flicker
Into the purloined pink lacy knickers

Running home on his last trip
Paulo held the pipe in a firm grip
The tortoiseshell inhaled the bong
Regardless of whether it was wrong
Though that night it seemed so right
Patsy his mistress looked at Paulo
In a mock gentle chide she said
'You're a badass guilty cat
You should be sitting on
Not stealing a "Welcome" mat'
Yet Paulo looked kind of pleased
Patsy laughed and gently teased
Sharing a language without words
Each knowing what the other heard
Paulo said to Patsy with feline glee,
'Hey man, you're right, you, me,
The whole world, we're all guilty'

Together they laughed and laughed
Not caring if someone blew the gaff
Their life and love was grasped forever
They swooned within a blue moon graph
The moment was too loose to lose
A star-filled feeling beyond the blues
Acting as if they were runaway lovers

A skeleton key to life they discovered
Patsy and Paulo caught as rebel-poets
Finding what mattered between words
Living within each other's open heart

The feeling was too raw to forget
Long into the star-kissed filled night
Together their lifeline love took flight

Please pass the Sandwich

The women met each week
To swop a few pleasant stories
Of how their lives panned out
And all their shared past glories
They had known each other for years
Seeing each other's involuntary tears
When the animals they cared for were abused
And still held by an invisible truce
Then when no one came to claim them
On their last day they paid their way
Being put down as a spare unwanted stray

They rehearsed and repeated
Their feelings for the creatures
And all the bulletins that featured
Multiple-abuse week-in week-out
Made their blood boil and hearts shout
Abandoned and ill-treated
Every form meted and discarded as detritus
Yet they claimed they are so 'like us'

Or so they said and meant
Their words shared and never bent
They talked of hating all animal abuse
How they cared for the welfare
Of the creatures that featured
As each new batch arrived
With food and feeling
Caring and sharing their lives
With those who had no worth
Because they were cursed by birth

She hated how they were treated
As worthless wastage and baggage
Their treatment was no less than savage
The strays ending up on a one-way voyage
Then Mary said to Margaret,
Can you please pass me a ham sandwich?
As it is the season of goodwill and fun
Would you prefer the turkey one?'

Prosopagnosia

The inability to recognise faces is a splendid gift
From some idol deity to give our lives an uplift
We can abuse animals from birth to death
Before they are born until their last breath
Cuddling the cute ones and eating the rest
Their arms and legs and right to their breast
Over and beyond those points in our favour
We can enjoy their company and yet savour
Each sweet and sour taste and their flavour
Morality is something we can simply sift
For god or some prophet has provided a gift
Ethics has no purpose and causes us no rift
We spend their lives using our daily thrift
So prosopagnosia is our best anaesthesia
An instant solution for abuse by amnesia
The swift gift we can use without a trace
No guilt or remorse of any sort in its place
As we forget the feelings with no disgrace
Forget who we killed in our consumer race
Yet without a mirror being near or anywhere
The corpse wears a look that reflects their fear
Created an ocean of hurt without a single tear
Our conspiracy that animals are our volunteers
Near their end we can play at being cavalier
Though we know we are impostor musketeers
For the first time we see in them a true base
A gift of an image of our human face
Seeing the problem we solved as our wirra
We avoided our lies by smashing the mirror

Pshaw he said to the Irish

The Irish have good reason to hate the English
Century-upon-century as victims of inhumanity
Soldiers ever-bolder in how they were treated
The bash bosh bish towards the biased English
Plus the wry smile of satisfying their vanity

In 2021 Stormont politicians had the chance
To ban hunting and let compassion advance
Especially as the English had provided a lead
The Irish had a straight aim in an open mind
A chance to prove animal abuse was left behind

Yet the numbers were the crunch of the vote
Seeing hunted animals as a distorted reflection
Of their own limited value by the English
They voted in the ban 38 for and 45 against
When the voiceless were dished by the Irish

GBS said 'pshaw' and he is one who knows
He spoke loudly from an unforgiving grave
His voice more serious than even his life itself
Seeing he knew first-hand all about the English
How animal life would be squandered not saved

The Irish became a sad imitation
Of their forever historical foes
Who put their country on the line
To render a fight or just surrender
Given this in the land of Behan
An echo of the Black and Tans
Against their bright fire and tune

With the rising of the rebel moon
Proving to be political poltroons
The Irish were crass and selfish
Making GBS even more waspish
Less a leprechaun and more elfish
Animal abuse was too hard to relinquish
Equally unequal as too weak to squish
Too tough for those morally vanquished
Proved to be much worse than the English
Shaw sure enough knows the Irish
Dyed in the wool as pale English
Just unjust and gonzo priggish
Lost in a maze of Delphic Gaelic

PTSD

The soldier risked his life and limbs
Wading in marked waters to the brim
Joined at the hip with his every task
His honest hound followed him around
Neither hiding feelings with a mask

On their return home the fever burns
In mines and minds learned and spurned
The soldier still screams as if still at sea
Nightmare scenes that will never cease
While his silent friend shares his misery

Together they earned their lowly fee
A high price paid for a forever PTSD

A desperate mother cries in the Home
In her hour's need she stands alone
Her baby snatched for someone to adopt
Each life cut short and each soul cropped
In an instant their two hearts are stopped

A cow sees her new-born calf in a stall
In moments while she can hardly crawl
They steal her calf from her protection
The men with money use a predilection
A baby and calf split as if by vivisection

Together they earned their lowly fee
A high price paid for a forever PTSD

The mother and baby and cow and calf
Cast asunder as a tempest sea cuts two in half
Each tossed and lost and double-crossed
By us content to forget to count their cost
On our crowing compost in a permafrost

Together they earned their lowly fee
A high price paid for a forever PTSD

A door of a Home and gate of an abattoir
Revolves as each new-born is abandoned
A future destroyed and yet unquestioned
Such stolen lives which fixes each destiny
All are carved without an epitaph PTSD

Rape of the Wild

It's a beautiful day
Let's go out and kill something

Hey children come and gather round
Lust is the lesson you will learn
From a whisper to a roar hear the sound
Of the season for killing and the reason our fire burns

Hey children come closer this time
Let the race towards his fate start
A thrill's a thrill and he's well past his prime
So soon you will see the scared stag's still-warm still-
beating heart

There's a blood-red sky kissed by a passing cloud
Blood on the lips of the circus crowds
Blood on the teeth of the unleashed hounds
Blood in the bubble that traps his voice
Blood on the blade that destroys his choice
Blood on his forehead is the child's prize
Blood on our hands when the bullet flies
Matches the bloody fear-filled light from the hart's dying
eyes

Hey children this is your moment
The price of life is a cheap death
Let this day stay and silently ferment
Within you so you will live your lust through the beast's
last breath

It's a beautiful day
Let's go out and kill truth

Red River Running

The government claim
They will quit culling
After a few more years
So voters and supporters
And mad Stag-spanners
Will have no reason for tears
Quelling their confused fears
No one will need
To have a troubled thought
Float across a mixed-up head
The government will fidget
As they run out of targets
Before they run out of lead
Though a new one will be bred
From all the rest
That we can deem a pest
So we will need more caskets
For all the extra culprits
We name in our next junket
However we fudge it
To add to the budget
As all the mines are closed
Honey bees and the land
We will kill by an overdose
All our toxic rivers
Will be deadly still
Yet shallow and running red
As the last gasping badger
No longer on political probation
And no need for her perturbation
For the river is her grave

Running and spreading red
As each marked bullet sped
So her life is shed
Spread on a river bed
Just as we always willed
Stilled with a blood rivulet
A bullet lodged in her head
She lies filled with our lead

Robots Never Bleed

The metal detector vivisectionist
Bent over the nameless exhibit
Stretched by a strap in a steel trap
Unable to resist the gibbet
The only sound to be heard
An echoed rattle without a word
From the exhibit's clamped teeth
Fixed in fear with a forced grin
Waiting for the end of the pain
Waiting in pain in vain again
Waiting for no reason but to die

A vivisectionist held the moving tool
A tool twisting and turning on a tool
The metal scarred the exhibit
Whose voice-box was removed
She mimicked e mimicked a goldfish howl
A fear-filled face without a growl
Probed from her heart to her bowel
Advances are red-hot
The scientist is a robot
The robot only rusts
The animal bleeds and dies
Then returns to ashes and dust

Her tool took the tool's life
A plight forfeited by our right
To plunder and rent asunder

Those fed our drugs to die
Scared mongrels lined up to fry

Four and twenty pigeons in a pie
The needle nails our every lie
As science serves to paralyse
Animal exhibits their scapegoat prize
Another death not worth a sigh
A new scientist no one could defy
A new scientist no emotion to deny
A new scientist whose circuits lie
Yet spills no tears or blood
A death with no reason to decry
Robots neither bleed nor cry

Salt of the Earth

Humaneness is not a dead external precept,
but a living impulse from; not self-sacrifice,
but self-fulfilment:

Henry Salt: *The Creed of Kinship*

The Arch was a man and a half
Saw what was real and was not
The time he spent in England
Where he learned points he never forgot
There and then he started on his journey
Towards the blinding light of compassion
Searching through the words of Salt
He dismissed deceit as his default
Compassion was as solid as granite
Never open to compromise or lies
Never open to an easy somersault
Soon realised it was the strongest suit
The diamond had no value he preached
It was the heart that had to be reached
What he was taught he had to teach
Whether black gay gender or otherwise

Killing animals was the losers' prize
Whatever is their voice and choice
Whatever reason they have to rejoice
There is no difference in how dignity
Holds a mirror for the living and dead
As all the blood that flows from each
Is born and dies a purer shade of red
The Arch was never parched of thirst

For the bubble of rights Salt had burst
Taught him animals were not knackwurst
They could live with or without us
Their own feelings equally valid first
In or out of court more sapient than most
Salt saw the vision behind habeas corpus
The same lifeblood flowed freely in all of us

For a feeling of flying freedom
Starched in heaven as on earth
Proof of a living value and worth
Animals have their place in heaven
An epistle that is natural and too true
Whatever colour and shape of their face
Animals are not some wild deuce ace
But reserve and deserve their place
To preserve a place in their life's race
Land and sea and sky is their space
As with Salt running with The Arch Tutu
Equally while they live on the earth too
Salt had a sense of their sentience
Matched by a fevered conscience
That sailed and surpassed silence
The Arch saw the reason to exalt
Those within the clarion call of Salt
His precision of vision shared by The Arch
An unassailable truth mixed with humour
Avoiding false rumour to find a pneuma
In even a parson or a pauper or a puma
Always guarded against the cannibal consumer
Salt looked through the eyes of another
Salt saw with prescience the sadness no less
Whether it was a hurt horse or his own mother

Scapegoats towards Slaughter

They line up ready
In an orderly queue
Into a death-swelling transporter
Denied a last meal
No reason to waste water
Noses out of wooden slats
To breathe before the splat
Eternal scapegoats for slaughter

In hunched pain together
In an orderly queue
Idly whacked by bloody sticks
By bored spattered workers
Arriving at a dark backwater
Their impatience caught her
With no time for any shirkers
Eternal scapegoats for slaughter

They line up ready
In an orderly queue
Forced to emit their last snorter
Then tipped upside down
Their throats slit amid a pumped aorta

A ritual religion bought her
A dying fixed face frown
Eternal scapegoats for slaughter

No more orderly queue
No one to support her
Our profits rise above water

With each drowned animal
Eternal scapegoats for slaughter
The plimsoll line of suffering
As every animals' offering
We borrowed from religion
A scapegoat and a stool-pigeon
Blaming animals for our acts
Escaping evidence and facts
Use trite wisdom as a sapient saw
Relying on religion as hard law
Eye-for-eye except it is easy to defy
If you do not need to see eye-to-eye
Moreover neither is it tooth-for-tooth
For how can a carcass decry the truth?

When it comes to killing a stranger
If it is someone who is not your kind
Another species is seen as a money-changer
We use a Nelsonian eye to feign being blind

Schrödinger's Cat

I hate water said the carp to the old trout
Who asked him what's that all about
You can't hate the thing that lets you live
Except when it is only take and not give
Wherever I move
Every river I travel through
There is never a safe place
When I am just swimming for food
All I find are barbed hooks in my face

I hate the sky said the wren to the bee
Who asked her why when you are free
Surely you can't hate your painted home
Yes but said the sickened bird
It is not what you have heard
Whenever I fly be it sunshine or rain
When I am only searching for a worm
I have to dodge bullets aimed at my brain

I hate the land said the pheasant to the farmer
Who asked him surely that cannot be true
You can't hate the space where you were born
It's easy for you but I have a reason to mourn
When I am going for a daily stroll
Rather than letting me roam free
I am attacked by gun-toting peasants
Intent to fulfil their wish to kill me

I hate the world said Schrodinger's cat to Atlas
Well how about that the seer said
As her thoughts began to swirl

As double-edged as a curved cutlass
I wonder how you can feel that way
When you have everything you need
That may seem true to you said the cat
But what you do not know
Is the hurt inside we cannot hide
My world is darker than dark
My search for shelter is spare and stark
My future starts and ends on the run
At the point of a machete and a gun
As abandoned as a church child bride
You have made my world a turning tide
No way forward and no way back
No exit or entry to your cul-de-sac
My world is a track on the road to suicide
Worst of all is your one-way ticket ecocide

Schrodinger's cat was wise to the wiles
Of ways the world can destroy our head
Perhaps the cat was right that at present
At the same time the world is alive yet dead

Does our ecocide prove beyond doubt he was
Yet we cannot prove plain truth just because
Content with our intent being sure we can hide
A present future as planned by our own hand
From committing to killing the world by ecocide
While we fail to decide if it is better to die by
The rising tide pesticide or countryside homicide

Shafted By Fashion

Standing in your furs 'n' your feathers 'n' minks
Your Old Lady takes one too many drinks
Your Daddy is a lawyer who defends kinks
Your brother hangs around with all the finks
Oh boy! I'm shafted by your fashion
I'm laughing so much there's onions in my eyes
You're living proof love is just a spoof
And I wish you were shafted too

Standing in your leather and rainbow suede
All that you are wearing from lives betrayed
Tricked and trapped as part of your trade
Stained by a price that will never be repaid
Oh boy! I'm shafted by your fashion
I'm laughing so much there's onions in my eyes
You're living proof love is just a spoof
And I wish you were shafted too

A life based on a want you never need
A life patterned by a passion for speed
A life cursed being born with a bad seed
Try finding a fashion that fails to bleed

From finishing school to the servant's bell
An accent that chimes with a hangman's knell
A hand-me-down remnant to a ne'er-do-well
Visit the banshee when your head starts to swell
Oh boy! I'm shafted by your fashion
I'm laughing so much there's onions in my eyes
You're living proof love is just a spoof
And I wish you were shafted too

She fell down the Stairs

Although Jasmine and Jake
Were always on the take
They would never forsake
Their devoted pet Blake
Who was part of the family
Yet devotion did not pass
When seen by the local vet
Who raised a curious eye
As he examined her injuries
Peering at the clear screen
Shook his suspicious head
Given what he had seen
With a question that was lit
He could not ignore or forget
Evidence he could plainly see
A hidden history of Blake's injuries

He asked them as a pair
They answered together
As if with a practised story
A politician's sort of 'sorry'
Glossing over the accident
Proving how much each one cared
Her injuries were too hard to bear
On the verge of their television tears
An Oscar performance well prepared
In unison 'She fell down the stairs'

When the vet showed them the traces
Two faces went ashen as they could see
A glowing X-ray of her internal injuries

When Mabel first came to stay
She brightened up their every day
Yet in a short time things changed
They figured she seemed deranged
All she touched they had to rearrange
Her presence jangled on their nerves
Patience was less than she deserved
Patience vanished in a swift swerve
When they took Mabel to the hospital
The harassed doctor cast a critical eye
Her injuries were somewhat auspicious
The more he looked the more he was sure
The evidence was way beyond suspicious
He asked them as a pair
They answered together
As if with a practised story
A politician's sort of 'sorry'
Glossing over the accident
Proving how much each one cared
Her injuries were too hard to bear
On the verge of their television tears
An Oscar performance well prepared
In unison 'She fell down the stairs'

When the doctor showed them the traces
Two faces went ashen as they could see
A glowing X-ray of her internal injuries

They could not wait to choose
A name for their new-born son
J-J brought an end to their blues
Shared their bliss with everyone
Until his crying wore them down

J-J fell out of the cot onto the floor
Somehow crawled out of the door
Jasmine was certain J-J had crawled
Yet Jake was certain J-J simply fell
When their stories did not quite gel
The room filled with a lurking smell

The vet met the doctor who met the cops
They met a judge who pulled out the stops
With him the truth could not be fudged
Analysed the evidence much as any burglary
Choosing each pinpointed point for the jury
Who then delivered their verdicts of 'Guilty'

The misfortune of the falls
When nature and old age calls
Was brought into sharp focus
When they examined the locus
As she fell over her tortoiseshell
Together they tumbled as a pair
Granny and her pet on slippery stairs
Her worn slippers on their worn stairs
Head over heels caused them a scare
Nevertheless the doctor was quite fly
The judge was quick to probe and pry
Judging them with a certain gimlet eye
The jury heard the tale from the pair
Seeing through their story on the stairs
Judged their evidence stretched credence
Their tale of a peculiar repeat coincidence
Of an animal or child or vulnerable person
In a confined situation one always worsens
Reflected and convicted by the verdicts 'Guilty'

After the verdicts the judge delivered wise advice
He trusted would be of value in future for a life:
'Be wary and slow unless you live in a bungalow
If you see a smile signifying something sinister
Be sure to hold on for dear life to the banister
Beware of the danger of being caught unawares
By people loitering with intent at the top of stairs
Especially a pair claiming to care in their liar's lair'

She sure suffers Shell-Shock

Grab a shell and throw her in the pot
Make sure the water is boiling hot
Turn it up so bubbles and steams
Change the shade of a black blue shell
The culinary creep can quit his dreams
When the colour changes to a pink hell
As she tries in vain to wriggle away
From the white-hot fountain spray
That burns through to boil her alive
A palette of pain makes the customers
Just clap and laugh at the bubbling jive
The owner calculates the profit and loss
It is just what every customer wants
There is no loser for the restaurant
When you are dealing with pure dross
The sound as her crisp shell breaks
Making his teeth tingle and gums ache
Enamel on edge as her shell cracks
Arms and legs and a bulbous back
She almost sates his appetite as he reached
For the last part of her broken carapace
Without any for him to be shamefaced
Seeing an image he all but screeched
Suddenly he felt his fingers on fire
As the flesh melted off all his bones
He groaned and moaned and was thrown
By the agony the heat piled upon his thumb
He imagined how it must have felt for her
Caught in that faraway moment of
Between a fraudster and a mobster
For no reason except a wasted taste

Checked his fingers and red guilt ridden face
Setting the immolation of an innocent lobster

He dwelt on the force of the mallet
Her pain outweighed by his palate
Much as every third-class gangster
Justifies his absence of conscience
With his secret cliched inner voice:
'I only killed people who deserved it'
The momentary lapse of filling his belly
Reconciled by his dwelling on Machiavelli
He smiled inwardly as he clicked
His bony fingers and made his choice
Choosing to be a heavy-headed mobster
When dealing with his captured lobster

Shylock's Blood

What is so special about black people anyway?
Was what the politician asked
But he did not remain long enough to find an answer
What is so special about black people anyway?
Was the question that fell from his lips
But he always thought too much thought was a cancer

What is so special about women?
The priest asked as if he was still in confession
Though he was far from the box of silence
What is so special about women?
He used communion to abuse every choirboy
As a daily distraction from his own violence

What is so special about speciesism?
Asked all the anti-social protesters
As they marched and waved placards and swore
What is so special about speciesism?
When the confederate flags were unfurled
As they asked for a T-bone and demanded more

Then out of the crowd
A voice cried out loud
As a fishmonger bull without a bullhorn
He stood tall and proud
Not caring if it was allowed
And then declared 'I wish I was never born'

You have treated me as if I did not matter
Injecting malice in blunder land
As if I had no value and I am one to batter

My eyes hurt too and my heart bleeds blue
And my mind and pulse and soul
Beats fast with a blood that pours
The bleeding cuts me to the core
The rain of pain makes me roar
Yet Shylock my heart is the same as yours

Silence of Science

Without research there would be no vaccine
It is essential we use research as our routine
The vaccine is the answer to the pandemic
If it means sacrificing a few million animals
Well rest assured that is purely academic
As for saying that our abuse of animals
Is the reason we created the pandemic
Well that is an idle misguided polemic
Like a burglar blaming the bank
For holding too much cash
When the disease is merely a backlash
Against our dash to treat animals as trash

Yet two questions continue to cause us congestion:
If animals are the same as us
What is our moral answer to causing them pain?
If animals are different to us
What is our moral purpose in causing them pain?
It seems that maybe the law
Is meant to protect the vulnerable
Yet when it came to slaves
The law found it to be tolerable
Century-upon-century make it comparable
But the law still finds the justice question
Equally easy to ignore as if it was unanswerable

Yet the answer to our quest
For a cure for every disease
Is to vivisect a million victims
Too vulnerable to resist
Why forfeit a gift of a monkey or a horse

When following Mengele is our best course
And try another experiment
On things we own too weak to prevent
An injected needle of death as our intent
While our crooked silent science need
Catches the concentration camp creed
Where our morality is hooked and bent

Skewer the Skies

Emmett Till was stilled and brought down
By a pack of cloaked cult clowns
Hiding behind their hoods of hate
He could not escape from their fate
Towards the nature of his birth
For them he had no value or worth
He was placed in a race he could never win
Emmett Till was killed at will due to his skin

Rem'mie Fells had a tale that tells
How prejudice in action smells
When the cop with the burning gun
Aimed and shot to kill 'another one'
With no way to retreat or re-track
Rem'mie was felled pell-mell
Because she was a woman born black

A cold blooded cop was hot on the trail
Of a man whose life was up for sale
At a knock down price below the pale
Too much trouble to take him to gaol
Chauvin held him tight in the gutter
Kneeing his windpipe to stop his mutter
For more than 500 seconds
While his lifeblood drains as death beckons
Who cares about his shouts
'Please, I can't breathe'
Then he cried, 'Help me Mama'
While his life was unsheathed
Chauvin pressed even harder
Through teeth that seethed

As if holding a trapped animal
One who made the cops annoyed
His plea for mercy served
As an epitaph for George Floyd
He was part of America's bric-a-brac
Meeting three cops hunting in a pack
Given his crime he had no way back
A death sentence for being born black

Sadder than all the pleas for mercy
Was his desperate final plea
For his Mama could not save him
She had had her own date with destiny
The slaves forced to pick cotton
And the gains all ill-gotten
Should never be forgotten
For us they were animals in kind
We abused and sent to their graves
Though the change in 1865
Supposed to protected those still alive
Failed to protect our animal slaves
Then as now they never forgave
Losing a War as abuse was their reference
Whether the victim is an animal or a slave
For them there remains no difference

Let's poison all the trees and bees
Let's count the profit we will seize
Let's keep spraying a toxic pesticide
Let's destroy all of the countryside
Let's forget the squashed hedgehogs
Let's forget all the underdogs
Let's keep turning the biased cogs

Who cares and who counts the cost
Animals in bloody mud in our Holocaust

Save your idle words for the tumbrel to fill
Until you realise the ghost of Martha White is right
She still proves truth is more than black and white
Until you're ready to skewer the skies with sparks
Showering the world with the spirit of Rosa Parks

Don't wait for a death-bed confession
Like De La Beckwith the killer in 1955
Save for him Emmett would still be alive
So don't call me at all
Until you march in Medger Evers memory
Until you listen to George Floyd's final plea
Until you hear the shrill of each animal we kill
Until you're ready to save the next Emmett Till

Songbird

I used to hear the songbird
Singing in the morning
I used to hear her singing
Chirping without warning
I used to hear her song
Every day and all day long
It made me sing inside
Along with her fluting song

I miss her and think about her fate
Wonder why in the unfathomable way
That life works there was no reason
For her to lose to a vanity-stricken
Ego-driven narcissistic trophy hunter
Using her bullets as bait
With nothing to offer
But her contaminated hate

With any luck the next duck
She shoots from the sky
Will by chance land on her
And by surprise take her off-guard

As her ever-itchy finger
Still on the trigger
She pulls as he falls
Given fate can be fickle
So the hail of bullets
As she was forced to pull it
Is released on her genitals
All in all she had a lot of balls

All in all blows away her brains
At the same time as her balls

Stag-spanner Ambush at Wounded Knee

The Apache Bison surveyed the scene
Champing at the bit and mustard-keen
Seeing the desolation devil cavalry
Sharpening swords and war cry words
Along with pistols and random riflery
Each rival ready for some savagery

The Bison were on the horizon
Looking down on the long drop
Ready to deliver their poison
Seeing soldiers circled in sizzling billets
Waiting to pump their repeater bullets
The Bison knew were meant for them
The Bison knew were to be their requiem

The Stag-spanners grouped on the hill
Awaiting with the Geronimo scouts
Searching for the poised soldiers
Perched ready to take them all out
Watching for the gathering Bison
Rising on the hazy mirage horizon
They signalled to the Comanche Deer
Concealed behind the camouflage trees
Deep within the highest brambles
Keeping their hungry spirit alive
Among the swarming angry hive
Of wild-eyed Cheyenne Bees

Chief Cochise Stag lifted her foot
Towards the hidden Navajo Foxes
Hiding their brush in the bush

Preparing for their final push
While the signal passed down the line
From Cherokee Boar to Boar
Ready for the rush when they roared
A marauding band of Animals-of-War

Starting with a grunting chunter
The sound echoed around the ground
Instilling fear within the soldier hunters
Intending to wreak their wanton will
Fired dragons surrounding the wagons
As they charged towards the punters
Wild Dove saw the ones who hunted her
Full of fright they dropped their smoking guns
Seeing the marauding mass Apache hunters
They had an instant case of the severe suns

The smell of fear overcame them all
As hooves and legs and cloudy galloping paws
Thundered down on them as death's call
A mirror-image of Draconian Stag-spanner laws

Each and every hungry human hunter
Feeling they had nowhere left to hide
Their scared eyes timed to meet their demise
The pounding hounds ripped out their insides
Left them to rot in their skins on the lonesome field
Where once they stood proud now could only yield
So where they once stood they now died
Each and every hunter lay in their blood
Each and every Native Animal felt the flood
Flowing through their scorched veins
Seeing that justice was truth in action

Proclaimed in the hunters remains
In that moment the Native Animals knew
All they had done was exercise their will
To understand what for hunters was a thrill
To examine why their lives
Counted for little or nothing
In the soldier blues' eyes
Before their brutal death arrives

It was plain on the Plains for all to see
The glory of their epitaph on Wounded Knee
They understood what the hunters meant
By the unspoken thrill of the unfolding event
The longed-for scene that nothing could prevent
Stag-spanners scruples stayed crooked and bent

The Stag-spanners felt no pity
Killing for a cold revenge
As minds and hearts were singed
Stag-spanners as the Angels of Avenge
Picking up the guns scattered around
The debris on the blood-filled ground
Seeing the wounded hunters
Spread-eagled in a pungent blur
Amid a blood-pooled violent sea
Finished each one off with a bullet
As a final act of reverse mercy
Just to put them out of their misery

They said on the tombstone:
The undiluted truth plain to see
Of their human epitaph on Wounded Knee
Animals behaved worse than animals

Animals behaved just like animals
Yet they forgot what was seminal

The animals behaved like criminals
With strength that seemed superhuman
From start to finish they were inhuman
A lesson they learned from the humans

The cavalry lying head to head
Eyes closed forever in fear
As each warriors' kick struck
The vanquished ran out of luck
Just like every captured criminal
Just like every captured animal
Birth as a mark of guilt in the dark
No light in their fight for life's spark
There was one point that mattered
The criminal had committed a crime
Some lives were constantly battered
Some lives were simply shattered
Some received their dues to save time
Yet the Stag-spanners were shorn
Of any defence to their crime
A cardinal one of simply being born

The Sioux Badgers were up all night
They were still hankering for a fight
None of them were tired
All of them were wired
They could take on any cavalry dog
Easier than rolling off a floating log
So every baiter was just another hater
That deserved to be caught and served

Between the Badger's vice-like jaws
Who were sure they had a cause

For they thought and often fought
For their stranded lives
Until the terrier man arrives
Then they smashed each face
And laughed as is commonplace
Well now they had a lesson
Direct from nature's delicatessen
This time we are not messing
This is your final tender blessing
Like us before this is your last door
So as your destiny awaits be ready to die
It is too late for your bleeding pleading cry

The Seminole Beavers were at the bank
Ready to make the hunters' lives blank
Preparing to make them walk the plank
Seeing the Beavers made their hearts tank
Each was holding a sharp cleaver
Each red-hot with a red-coat fever
One-by-one the hunters simply fell
One-by-one into the drink and dell
Beavers clamped their feet on their teeth
Giving the hunters someone new to meet
The waters opened in a feral flood
Floating on top was their oily blood
Turning turtle as with the Beavers before
The hunters were knocking on hell's door
Their every last gurgle and bubble
As they bought the fruit of trouble
They had started in the avenging wend

Now they were there at their very end

Iroquois Hares hid in the hedge
Waiting just waiting on the edge
For the signal to be given to break out
For they were enraged waiting to clout
Every type and any kind of courser
Would soon be forced by him and her
Black Eagle gathered in a Crow battalion
Waiting as a bunch of palomino stallions
Hundreds of Hares as an animal army
Ready to course the cruel coursers
Ready to hang on their jutting jugulars
Poised to chase the long-time burglars
Then just when they least expected
They grabbed them around their prospect
With teeth sharper than they suspected
Nipped their member below the plimsoll line
As if it was a shrivelled cud for them to dine
Then when their victims' screams
Filled their daytime nightmare dreams
The army of Hares were unleashed
The hunters screeched and screeched
Yet the Hares were so taken with the gaff
Played it rough and tough
Figuring it was about enough
To make a Cherokee cat laugh

Blackfoot Squirrels made their play
Cyril the squirrel was made that day
It was a pure pleasure as he was grey
So unlike the much favoured red
The cavalry saw him as good as dead

But the scene was great
For the shock that lay in wait
As the reds and greys were best mates
They met on the battlefield wheels
Rolling as they took their last squeals
Then red Beryl joined the Squirrels
Even grey Daryl joined the Squirrels
They were neither feared
Nor worried by being scared
As they bounced around the fences
Ready to deliver the sentence
The air was heavy and intense
Stag-spanners striking out in self-defence

The Stag-spanners circled the wagons
While crouching hunters hid behind
A blind row of real-life snap-dragons
Praying the Angels would change their mind
As Apaches defending their land
In a way the hunters had not planned
With a force borne of revenge
Too late for them to scavenge
For the Trail of Tears centuries of abuse
Now the tables turned and fortune burned
Now they would not listen to any excuse
As they charged and killed the hunters
Seeing just a bunch of losing punters
Their victims' lives flashed by
In the wink of a changing sky

When the Apache Native Animals learned
Something that was of lasting concern
Why did hunters see their blood spilled

Was a befitting prize which just filled
Their hearts with a raw pleasure
To boast about their trophy treasure
Now all at once the Stag-spanners were shown
That which they never could have known
By stealing the hunters crooked will
Led to the war ambush's outstanding bill

The Apache Bison surveyed the scene
Awash with the spreading scarlet stream
Of spent bullets and swirling blood
Floating in a silver sea of misery
Mixing their last memories in the mud
So clear even the blind could see

The Apaches could answer the question
That had long foxed them all
Way past the auto-suggestion
That had led to the devil cavalry's fall
They discovered when forced to swallow
One more variety of life's bitter pill
It was not hard to follow
Though the truth was hollow

As the human blood
Flowed on and on in the mud
As hard as it was for them to say
As the bodies stayed where they lay
With no one left alive to dispute
The feeling of a prophet and a prostitute
The same in the game of each examined life
Between the afterlife and the wildlife
Exactly as the devil cavalry they slaughtered

From a fixed mind to a blocked aorta
Little White Dove became the hangman's daughter
From Blackfoot to Cheyenne each woman and man
Every tribe from Choctaw to Cree had a secret plan
That was now out in the open as they met Jim Crow
From Waco to Winnebago from Comanche to Crow
As the wild animal tribes bathed and basked
Seeking the answer they had all long asked
Their unvarnished wish and unleashed will
That sprung straight out of history's wisdom
Chief Legal Beagle Hawkwind of the Choctaw
Who had practised law and studied the legend
Of Plutarch and Pythagoras via a vestal Virgil
Discovered a truth that was a frozen codicil
They loved the sheer chilled thrill of the kill

They held a powwow to try and discover
Why the cavalry were intent on destruction
What they found in their pipes of peace
Made them wonder if they would ever cease
As demolition and death and spoils of war
Gave them more satisfaction than construction
When Little White Dove held the gun
Something lit within her
Making her totally undone
Before her closed eyes she realised
Balanced against the flame and function
Much as the cowboys wanted to destroy
She knew her tribe was snared too
By the sour-sweet seduction of destruction

Stag stands at Bay

The all-seeing albatross swooped above the sea
So you could all but read her mind:
'I swear if I could change places with the stag
I would and so put a bullet in the brain
Of the sour-hearted hunter
Whose blind mind bind would remain'

The one-eyed grunt hunter
Whose intent was to shunt her
Into the wild sea so she was free
Much as a helpless child in his spree
With one aim to claim as he hides
Behind his coward smirk pride
As a runt on a turnstile chain
Knowing in his buckled heart
He was only able to use his gun
To shrink his crooked soul
Because she stood at bay
Feared face of fright and flight
Wide-eyed as if she somehow knew
This was her to be her very last day

Her scared eyes dying within sight
Without effect on the blunt punter
Whose only aim was to stunt her
So she breathed less and no more

She looked wistful as if in prayer
Almost asking him to spare her
For if she could she surely would
Have joined her hooves to pray

Lest his intent was to rob her life away
Until the fetid-faced hunter
Was kissed by his rusty soul
Taking her body and mind as a whole
Taking aim he lodged lead deep in her brain

The all-seeing albatross swooped above the sea
So you could all but read her mind:
'I swear if I could change places with the stag
I would and put a bullet in the brain
Of the sour-hearted hunter
So only his blind mind bind would remain'
The albatross figured with no sense of dread
The dead-loss hunter would be no loss if dead
Yet with no widespread wish to harm or blague
The albatross saw her future in the fate of that stag

Statistics of Misery

Pump a pellet of poison through her
Jump her heart up to overload
Cast a chill for the cold-blooded kill
So her body starts to explode
Your answer to a cure for cancer
Always happens to be the same
Pick him as your next faceless victim
Just another number without a name

Millions and millions pile up in a stack
See the cash flow free from you and from me
Millions and millions pile up on the rack
See all our statistics of misery

Force-feed the dog one more overdose
Dressed to die he looks so depressed
Just one more pointless experiment
A truth the public won't have guessed
The scientist seeks another grant
To make the fat guinea-pig thin
Their violence concealed by their silence
While sad-eyed carcasses fill the trash bin

Fill the cat's tank with murky water
High enough to cover his eyes
As he tries to swim right to the brim
Only his corpse begins to rise
Funds that fill the professor's coffer
Injects every creature that moves
Kill the breeds for reports no one reads
A degree in suffering is all it proves.

Sticks in your Stomach

Save your disgust as your lust for foie gras
As a delicacy tingles on your tongue
Knowing the goose whose liver you gorge
Died in agony for your palate is strong
So save your moral stance as it is as subtle
As a vegan butcher without bottle
It is time to own up as a blood-sucking leech
Hiding a blacksmith's mallet to rupture a peach

Forget criticising the French
Wrestling your conscience wrench
When you scan the menu
Knowing all too well it is true
Your palate is the pliers twisting her fate
Marked out in chalk on the blackboard slate

There is no need to translate her destiny's date
In England you can eat legal cruelty on a plate

Smell their liver and swell your belly
You can find a reason via Machiavelli
Forget the girdled goose
She just drew a deuce
Every gob is her sluice
So her taste outweighs her suffering
Given the choice it is mouth-watering
So our taste outweighs her suffering

Stopcock and Bull

The crowd looks and waits
Their eyes fixed on the gate
Then it is flung open
So the huge bull escapes
Towards the sawdust Caesars
Naked Emperor plays Macbeth
So he charges towards the capes
But only towards his own death

The crowd waits with bated breath
Nostrils flaring ready for their fun
As they wait for him to bake
Beneath the burning cruel crisp sun
Counting the time it will take
Before he takes his very last breath

The cuadrilla removed his horns
To even up the odds in the fight
When the matador stabbed him
Knowing he was out of luck
With no horns to prick and hook
A coward with a ready-made victim

The picador parades around the arena
Tiptoes as a prancing ballerina
When he thrusts the sharpened darts
All around her fear-beating heart
Her cries make the crowd meaner
Laughing as she is their misdemeanour
The delirious crowd as a mass of hyenas

The matador catches the mood of the crowd
All their laughter and shouts echo so loud
Waiting for the spreading pool-spilled blood
Dancing with his dagger drawn in an ego-cloud

A bull bleeds in the sun-kissed run
As always it is a one-sided pendulum
So each one's life will be undone
Where the weight swings against the bull
Where hearts are vacant and minds are full
Of hate and pride in a bitter sour skull
Each one in the crowd
Each one with the sword
Finds a thrill in a cheap kill
While their hate is heard
Taking a life by cheaper words

The priests clapped and laughed
For too long and too loud
Locked in pride in a shroud
Until their hands bled with shame
Although they knew no one said
Their pained blood was the same
Shade as that that the bull shed

At Communion the next morning
Though there was no mourning
For it was and is only a bull
For the priest knows the prayers
He offers on the body and bread
Shared with such feeling
The thoughts still reeling
Through his muddled head

When he claps and claps
In every bull fight
Every day and night
His excuse another religious ruse
Being finally a bunch of bull Shiite
The priest looked at his hands
Saw the stigmata of the blood
Of every bull that he saw
Being tortured to death
His malice in his chalice
Struck him hard with a thud
He knew with conviction
He witnessed a crucifixion

The cuadrillas wander so proud
Applauded by the baying crowd
The subalteros dressed in silver
But the matador is clothed in gold
He grabs her ears and tail as trophies
An echo of the fox-hunting landscape
For the same reason as fruits of rape

The cry from the crowd is so loud
Every word can be heard
As a repeated crescendo 'Kill her!'
The torture is dressed up as culture
Proving why 'matador' means 'killer'
Then the English tourists all go home

From the start the method and the mood
Is to steal her heart and create a feud
Anything as long as the crowd is intrigued
And to make the odds even she was fatigued

Her weakness reflects the banderillo's strength
Plunging the darts into her
To dial into the crowd's wavelength

Then the picador begins to prance
And drives a lance into her
To satisfy the growing crowd
Of poseurs and voyeurs
Impatient for torture to recur
As the matador performs
With the frightened hooded
Snorting blindfolded horse
Dancing in the sand
With a handy harpoon in his hand
He drives it into her with so much force
The bull bellows and starts to collapse
And the matador jumps down and laughs
In time with the laughter and clamour
As the crowd waits
Impatient for death's dull glamour
While ever-hungry they clap and clap
The matador gives her one last angry slap
Her last gasp as she tries hard to rise
Then sinks and dies before their flint eyes

It is not a question of being squeamish
While the money pours into their coffers
From tourists who follow culture's offer
They gain from the English on arriving
Who tell tales on their roam back home
Glorify the sunshine in the English rain
While their taxes pays for the bulls' pain
Buying death is a pleasure

They learn to treasure
As a spectacle of leisure

Yet they dwell on the hate
Without any hope
When against their wish
If not their bulging purse
Yet when they say they find it perverse
Seeing a glimpse of their own hearse
They are intent not to discover
A truth as rare as an Eskimo in the Sahara
A truth hid by panda-ringed mascara
Proof of the ever phoney history trope
The English are a nation of animal lovers

Straight from the Horse's Mouth

Smack! Thwack! Whack!
Lash upon lash
Smack! Thwack! Whack!
Lash upon lash
The crack and the slash
The whip and the gash
Of course I'm just a horse
Screaming 'til I grew hoarse
Though I know in my gut what's true
So where are you now we need you, William
Wilberforce?

I'm Jonjo Jacknori
Riding's my story, chasing glory
I grip the whip and just let rip
That's my job, that's my joy
In my hands she's my whipping-boy
Sometimes it's a matter of life and death
Sometimes she stings as she takes her last breath
Beating the bookie by beating the horse
That's no reason for our remorse
Rest assured
We don't give a monkey's about a whipped horse
When it comes to winning we're all whores

Train a foal for our goal
Add a callus to her heart and soul
That's our job, that's our joy
She then becomes our whipping-boy
We want our rookie to beat the bookie
We forget each lash as we count the cash

If she dies the prize is still in our eyes
If she loses when Jonjo uses too much force
That's no reason for our remorse
Rest assured
We don't give a monkey's about a whipped horse
When it comes to winning we're all whores

I'm here to place a bet
So I won't fret about her cold sweat
If she trips from too many flips
Dies from too many whips
Well when her life's last race is run
We'll just find another one for more fun
And end hers by a quick fire stun gun
That's our final choice for every horse
That's no reason for our remorse
Rest assured
We don't give a monkey's about a whipped horse
When it comes to winning we're all whores

I'm here to take the bets
I just don't care how hard the race gets
That's what it takes, those are the stakes
In our game there's some strife
It's just a horse losing her life
After all that's just the way the rain falls
Her pain and our gain are the twin limb calls
Sometimes an unlucky heart somehow stalls
That's no reason for our remorse
Rest assured
We don't give a monkey's about a whipped horse
When it comes to winning we're all whores

We're here to play to win
She's a running machine, not our kin
I've invested all my money
I'm here for the honey
Really don't care about the whip
When it's lashed across her hot hip and lip
You expect me to care about a horse?
That's a kind of nonsense I can't endorse
That's no reason for our remorse
Rest assured
We don't give a monkey's about a whipped horse
When it comes to winning we're all whores

We want to light our fuse
Though we know horses are born to lose
Sometimes we're a little too loud
We're the drunk party crowd
Our passion her dash on the bend
A swift blip from the whip and she'll soon mend
Then it's the stable or on the table
If she's a slacker straight to the knacker
That's no reason for our remorse
Rest assured
We don't give a monkey's about a whipped horse
When it comes to winning we're all whores

Smack! Thwack! Whack!
Lash upon lash
Smack! Thwack! Whack!
Lash upon lash
Thrash across my eyes
Hurt so I couldn't rise
Still screaming from my grave

A dead thoroughbred slave
Of course I'm just a horse
My Code a silent Morse
Caught under the jockey's thumbscrew
My tombstone tells a tale that's true
So where are you now we need you, William
Wilberforce?

Straight from the Trainer's Fingers

Gordon Elliott is so photogenic
A model trainer on Morgan
It is a pity it is tragic
That he has no vital organ

Gordon Elliott puts up two fingers
And grinning as he makes a call
The frozen photo still lingers
The fat trainer astride his last fall

Gordon Elliott smiles from ear to ear
Captures a smile for the camera
The horse is the last thing on his mind
Between the shutter and slaughterman

Morgan earned cash for the man
He died on his gallops in 2019
Now one more dead horse can be seen
On the stilled Twitter screen RIP

Elliott will train another horse
Who will run and run of course
And if he loses his life at the source
Remember no one gives a monkey's
For like Morgan he is just a horse

Elliot sits with all his weight
Sprawled across the dead horse
Showing contempt rather than remorse
For being caught by the camera's glare
Perhaps it would not matter

If it was just a donkey
Then Elliot's fate would less
As it would be one more flunkey

Strike Some Sparks

Rubin Stacy sways in the breeze
Sheriff's men stare at his knees
Sheriff's men kick up the leaves
Rednecks loiter under the trees
Then they pulled the loose noose tight
His eyes popped and filled with fright
Rubin Stacy swings in the breeze
Stray dog suspended at his knees
Truth is always forged under fire
A mask won't change the face of a liar
Stacy and the stray couldn't win
Rubin was pinched and lynched for his ebony skin

Don't call me at all
I don't buy your lies
Save your second-hand stories
And don't try to philosophize
Just heed my need
A message that's short and stark
Only call me when you're going to
Raise some sparks for the ghost of Rosa Parks

Maya Angelou learned as a child
The smile of the paedophile
Was a leer meant to beguile
And break a mind free and fragile
Filling her with promised fear
Forced her voice to disappear
No less than a sin and a crime
Maya was betrayed for all time
Just a girl and her dog on the street

She heard the stalker's pounding feet
She heard the caged canary sing
Maya was broken without a prayer or a wing

Don't call me at all
I don't buy your lies
Save your second-hand stories
And don't try to philosophize
Don't call at all
Until your bite matches your bark
Only call me when you're going to
Raise some sparks for the soul of Rosa Parks

George was grabbed by stone cold Chauvin
A pack with a biased plan
Handcuffed George under their van
Bad blood while his race almost ran
George winced with each wave of pain
Chauvin burst his windpipe vein
George choked and cried 'please, I can't breathe'
Chauvin's death knell knee wove the wreathc
From 1619 'til its High Noon
America burns its biased moon
George Floyd was destroyed by the pack
Sentenced to death for his crime of being born black

Please don't shame my name
I'm deaf to your lies
I can't use your false excuse
And don't try to philosophize
Burn bright and right
A torch of truth our trademark

Only call me when you're going to
Raise some sparks for the heart of Rosa Parks

Let's poison all the honey bees
Think of the profit we'll seize
Keep spraying that pesticide
Let's destroy all the countryside
In the end it won't matter
Let the fat cats get fatter
Don't avoid ritual slaughter
Or avoid the polluted water
So let's all live high on the hogs
With 'no blacks, no Irish, no dogs'
Who cares and who counts the cost
8 million horses lost in our World War Holocaust?

A truth that don't offend
Is not one to defend
So just leave me alone
Let me pick another bone
Don't call at all
Unless you're ready to save the shark
Then call me when you're going to
Strike some sparks for the spirit of Rosa Parks

Strike some sparks for the ghost of Rosa Parks
Strike some sparks for the soul of Rosa Parks
Strike some sparks for the heart of Rosa Parks

Stripping Stripe

Stripe was starving to death
Scattered seeds were too few
All the nuts had long gone
She flew onto the bird bath
To claim a drop of water
The builders' sine qua non
A new-build site stole her home
Nothing was left to support her
No food and nowhere to roam

She tried to lift the bin
Where the scraps were hid
The owner called her a 'psycho'
When she made him let her go
She bit him to get at the waste
A temptation of imagined taste
Was enough to keep her alive
Stale scraps to help her survive
She jumped onto the garden table
Spying food as if a treat in a fable
She bit the man holding her arm
A building site that was a former farm
Now branded as determined vermin
She balanced as a clothes line stranger
But unwelcome as a diseased danger
Caught in our trap as nature's cur
Neighbours used it to kidnap her
A prelude to their neighbour feud
To stop her hunt for discarded food

Trying to survive while barely alive
Where red is dead truth is dark and dense
An accused grey squirrel has no defence

The wandering homeless man
Held his head in his hands again
Then broke into the bungalow
To steal the bread and cheese
Without the time to ask or beg
With no one to make contact
To say 'please' or show respect
Though it was old and stale
He entered the garden at his peril
He was another kind of squirrel
Then the old homeless stranger
Ended up cold in a barred cell
Society's vision put him in prison

Paws squeezing through the gap
Bleeding paws caught by the trap
Starved dehydrated their hate sated
When her fight for food failed
She was held by steel teeth and nailed
While he only ended up in gaol
Rather than dead he was at least fed
Unlike her he was nature's red
A new home though not his own
It was a place to rest all the same
One of the two to wake up again

It is said 'Better red than dead'
Perhaps more significant that day
As an epitaph for a nomadic grey

When the barbecue smoke flew high
From one they determined was vermin
Her starvation dismissed as a false alibi
Red blood stained her grey dead eyes
As obese neighbours gorged on squirrel pie

Syphilis in Tuskegee

Their conspiracy cabal thrived
Infected victims and their wives
The children lost their lives
Others disabled and born blind
Died in agony before their time
A sign proved the one-line track
The doctors to a man were white
While every single victim was black

Nazis formed their intent from the start
Smashing each Jewish mind and heart
Denying them any comfort or a bed
Standing huddled in a railway shed
Transported when they ran out of luck
Freighted women and children and men
Day and night packed tight in cattle trucks
Awaiting fate by a visit from Death's Angel
In the shape of a butcher-vivisector Mengele

Doctor Sims in Tuskegee never met Mengele
The vivisector-butcher had never heard of Sims
Yet the two doctors shared a cruel common craft
Each one had practised their profession on animals
Graduated to be charlatan craftsman criminals
Each seduced by power over powerless as their key
A guarantee no one in their grasp would ever be free
Vulnerable wounded and wasted to die without liberty
There was no reason for scientists to stick with animals
When with ease they could experiment on you and me

In England the ideas filtered into Porton Down
Where those standing up were soon put down
War was the reason the soldiers were in pain
War was the reason pigs were put in the frame
Their skin was so close to soldiers using a gun
Who were wounded heroes hit by an enemy gun
Shot in battle with their life and death on the run
Now the pigs too had run out of luck
Each pig looked at the cocked rifles
As they had seen the scientist as a friend
Until their echoing squeals were stifled
A repeat bullet-round signalled each pig's end

Some were penniless
All were powerless
No selection between a sinner and a saint
Prejudice unleashed was without restraint
Once grasped by every medical Nazi asp
No one could ever be free
Every doctor delivered the dosed disease
Law and morality lost in a deep-freeze
Slaughter of the innocents by syphilis in Tuskegee
400 men for 40 years tortured by science immorality

Now is not the time to shake a head and mutter tut
There never was and never is a reason to pussyfoot
Yet let us not seek our reason to only condemn them
For animals their per diem at our hands is their requiem

The Animal Rebellion Hellions

We are the Animal Rebellion
We are the new rage hellion
We are calling out animal abusers
We are here as your human accusers
We are the ghost of Animal Rebellion

We are the Animal Rebellion
We are the new rage hellion
We are the voice for those denied a human tongue
We are their voice to stop them being stung
We are the ghost of Animal Rebellion

We're here to free prisoners from your pens
We're here to protect and save all our penned friends

We are the Animal Rebellion
We are their hell-bent hellion
We are their planet battalion
We're wilder than a roped stallion
We're their genesis and your nemesis
We are the first and last Animal Rebellion

We are the Animal Rebellion
We are the new rage hellion
We'll show you what a band of men and women'll do
We're targeting all the criminals too
We are the ghost of Animal Rebellion

The Animals Film Framed

Let the skinny-ribbed dog keep barking
At the last abandoned caravan
The tight rope walker stole the elephant
Who cried non-stop on seeing the man
Ah but do I care
The ringmaster hit disaster ended up in plaster
Tripping over the prancing horse troop
Pierrot traded all the tears of a lifetime
For all the lions he had long since duped
Selling the monkeys as the circus moved on
As the last act of their unravelling betrayal
Unleashed a nightmare feel too strong to conceal
As *The Animals Film* started to freeze over
On the broken-down spinning reel-to-reel
The tragedy is over let the comedy begin

Bring on the dancing bears
Serve up my head on a plate
The Saturnalia is over
I have really lost a hold on fate
Ah but do I care
The Fat Lady's mirror shows the effigy
Of a stuffed hunted weasel and a wren
And the face has a trace of a sly smile
With a mean wish to meet crooked men
Estragon has been waiting in vain so long
He has faded into a neo-confessional den
The rebel-poet's wound will never heal
As *The Animals Film* is frozen forever
On the broken-down spinning reel-to-reel
The comedy is over let the tragedy begin

The Animals War of Independence

No kindred soul in chained Jim Crow
No Mississippi Chinese Compliment
No whip on his much-marked back
No whip on the horse on the track
No hanging on the Strange Fruit tree
No gallows for the stray dog born free

Forget your tired lies to fire us
With half-baked ideas on a virus
So the vaquita slowly dies
To satisfy your trumpet lies
Ringing on a cure by medicine
Between your crime and cardinal sin
Between the lines of Manchu Wuhu
Drying your wet markets is overdue
Even you know your claims are untrue
Damn your wet markets damn you
With your blood-curled flag unfurled
Locking poached pets in your underworld

Save your lies for someone
Who will listen and even believe
Anyone who is easily deceived
While you christen lies as forsooth
Our tongue touches your gnawing tooth

No religious ritual slaughter
No barbed hooks in the water
No wet market Pinnochio
No more buffalo Custer blow
No kindred soul in chains

No plate carcass remains
No dog-whistle Jim Crow

The Blackboard Jungle

The teacher told the class
About Darwin and the mass
Of creatures he discovered
Who were in so many ways like us
Existing to survive no less than Dreyfus
It was a lesson worth learning
Experiments of our yearning
Information we gain from vivisection
With no harm to us and no objection
Their pain our gain to remain sane
Said the teacher as he explained
How we have won by a self-selection
When a boy at the back of the class
Who rarely asked a single question
And if asked answered 'pass'
Who everyone branded a dunce
Because of what he did once
When he was very young
Thereafter soiled and spoiled by bias
Raised his hand and shyly asked:
'Sir, if they are the same as us
Why do we treat them as such rubbish
Just to use and abuse and put them in zoos?'
The teacher prepared a set text to spout
To prove the boy was typically confused
With no idea what he was asking about
Characteristically based on his intellect
In turn based on a 'C' stream selection
It would not be hard to fool him
With benefits we gain from vivisection
The child became tongue-tied and silent

While he waited for the teacher to mumble
When the bell rang to end the life lesson
Leaving the question in dusty fading chalk
Where logic and lies take a literary tumble
As the noisy class left the blackboard jungle

The Bonds of Birth

The lesson of their lives
As birth and death arrives
We are descendants of Epstein
Practised in wiles of Weinstein
Caught and bartered and bought
Sold in our legal slavery
Especially by you and me
False words of welfare
Proof we do not care
For we own their world
We own the rocks we hurl
Then if it matters we rat on her
Worthless patter serves to shatter
As mean as Epstein and Weinstein
Stand in the shadows mouthing spleen
It is our earth that binds the bonds
Their birth we weigh for our worth
Killing bees to seize their honey
Killing trees to gather more money
Sell their birth to destroy their earth
Kissing goodbye to a blind eye-tooth
As valid as a practised Putin truth
Self-appointed victors stalk the earth
Possessing yet eating the purloined cake
Finished at the start by our volcano heart
Then dwell as they ache and are forsaked
We aim to break the bonds of their birth

The fat cat lab Rat

Who wants to wear a wig or a hat
When it is so much easier to kill a rat
To the background wail of Fake Fat
A cure for baldness is where it's at

Forget the fact we are all obese
Feeding our faces with midnight feasts
Any reason we can use we will seize
While the growing rodent bodies freeze
We do not care what you allege
We are all living life on the ledge
Drinking to excess takes us to the edge
A daily promise to take the pledge
Instead forget a feckless promise
A rat's life is the thick end of our wedge

We all snort the snow white horse
Lawyers and lovers sharing each curse
Junkies in alleys shoot up with force
Kill a million rats as a matter of course

We can do what we like as it is only a rat
The same as choking a mangy stray cat
Or eating a pangolin or a wild captive bat
Experiment on anything all day in the lab
The place for another bat and cat and rat
Put them up with the pigs then rat-a-tat-tat

We poison them as our tasters
To protect us as greedy wasters
Lest we get fatter is all that matters

Get the gat so their insides go splat
Bullets or gas or listening to Fake Fat
Anything as long as we do not get fat

The First Thing we do is Kill all the Lawyers

The animals figured enough was enough
No longer prepared to accept such stuff
Now the gloves were well and truly off
Way past the time to start playing rough
So all at once the whippoorwill
Gave a shrill no tongue could quell
Every last one in the crowded Courtroom
Gathered all their strength together
They knew it was now or never
Their lives could only be saved
If they were prepared to sever
The complete caboodle tongues of liars
By taking a lesson from Shakespeare:
The first thing we do is let's kill all the lawyers

Then that is precisely what they did
As the roles were reversed for all time
Without a sheltered port in the storm
When the battle-cry went up as primed
Each struck with an arrowed heart
Every animal there took them apart

With strength and soul and blood pumping
Red-hot topsy-turvy and high jumping
Straight from their thumping multiple-hearts
Proving the liars and lawyers were the same
Equally they knew that they were all to blame
Each in their own way descendants of Descartes

As the Lord Chief Justice breathed his last
He asked with a plaintive plea: 'Why me?

What have I ever done except tried to be fair?'
'Ah' answered the pig with a sarcastic snort,
'This is just us with our own sense of justice
Indulging in a kind of payback-time sport
You are in our arena and we make the rules
So all humans are imprisoned in our fort
We are no longer your plaything tools
There is a feeling called belief we lost long ago
We learned the thief is a judge in a new robe
We are taking back everything you pilfered
As the self-appointed ghost of Dick the Butcher
This is your first and last visit to the future
Now is the time for us to blow you a mort
As the first criminal in our Kangaroo Court'

The Fish who failed to Scream

He threw the line that fooled the fish
The rusty hook caught the bream
He could hardly see her struggle
Part of the joy of his serene dream
As he overcame her strength
By the rising line and his length
Catching her silver scale in the stream
He was secretly glad fish do not scream

The bent hook curled around her throat
The time was right for his lucky strike
Close on the surface he grabbed her
The prize was a splashing thrashing pike
He found her fight added to the delight
Using his power and all his might
Catching her silver scale in the stream
He was secretly glad fish do not scream

He threw the lasso into the river
Intent on catching another carp
His jagged hook and line and sinker
Reflected his mind blunt and sharp
Like the last throw of a cardsharp
Wanting to make sure he got that carp
Catching her silver scale in the stream
He was secretly glad fish do not scream

Intending on ending with a perky perch
He stood close to the fast water's ledge
His line got caught in a drooping birch
That dragged him to the snagged edge

Losing balance he slipped on the bank
A crooked hook in his tongue as he sank
Angler and line swinging in the stream
Both gripped beneath the vice slipstream

Beneath the water open-mouthed
Bubbles killed his fish-like shout
The perch was dragged down and out
While the angler was dragged all about
The spreading pain shot through him
His life flashed in a nightmare scheme
Echoed by his heart-rending scream
Followed by scream-after-scream
In that moment he lost all doubt
About the cold-fish-no-pain shout
The angler so often used to spout
A different time and a different theme
Drowned as if he was another bream
Sinking as no one heard his stifled scream
Like catching her silver scale in the stream
His pumping heart went boom-boom-boom
Seeing the crashing flashing watery tomb
No longer secretly glad fish do not scream

The Good Death

They have lived a good life
The trade off for being born
Followed by giving and living
Not unlike an auctioned wife
Or a slave now in her grave
After all she too is in a cage
No need to work for a wage
The bargain we have struck
Until she runs out of luck
Is to get fatter and fatter
How could obesity matter
It is a philosophical trainer
Nothing is clearer or fairer
Nothing is sounder or saner
Then again the same goes for her
When stripped naked for her fur
No different than her cuddly child
Who we rescued from the wild
Now he is finger-feeding tame
At my expense so it makes sense
When he grows fatter so easily
Now in his prime it is his time
As with his mother before him
Turning the final funeral page
Their lives shared by our sage
Plus a sprinkling of our thyme
As ever it is as a matter of fact
Almost a known unspoken pact
It is as if she knew her fate
It is as if he knows his fate
From the moment I grabbed her

Her proper place was on my plate
My money for her life was the key
Unlocked the deal to feed my family
The final test of what matters is real
Living a good life to dying a good death
Measured by how it makes us feel
No one alive could object to that deal
Even the one who provided our meal
I swear she was happy until her last squeal
I really miss her although her race was run
Yet we are keeping her memory in the family
Now I am looking forward to our next meal
Fortunately for us it happens to be her son

The Horsemen of Hate

Why is it so hard for you to see
That the sum of the misery
Adds up to the acts
Of those whose repose
Is only a change of clothes
The Naked Emperor wore
In the guise of Custer's bribery
While you wallow in the luxury
You find in a closed soul
Combined with a perfect blind mind?

A horseman of the apocalypse
Whose message is lost on your lips
Until it is far too late
For will we ever realise
Even as our bullets make the sky cry
We will still close our eyes
Using lies as our angling bait
As the five horsemen of hate

Salt 'saw deep in the eyes of the animals
The human soul look out' upon him
Borne of a wisdom he has seen and known
Yet we rest on every whim
Of any fanciful notion
Making every one our victim
While we fail to vault
Our fault in the vision of Salt
We know the eyes of a horse
Reflects his image and our own
A truth we have tried to divorce

314

The law of Italian Love

The government of Italy
Have granted their citizens
A legal concession to kill seven doves
A key to the prison of hate over love

A law that takes their hard hearts
And fits as neat as a chain-mail glove
A politicians' note to catch a vote
By a show of the democracy of love

A grand stance for their citizens
Against the local flying denizens
Nothing could be better
Than being a political pace-setter

For them to be always thinking of
The lasting route towards democratic love
As neat and sweet as a Mafia blastoff
Is a mass killing of the white peace dove

Where all gangsters proliferate
At their palace of wisdom gate
Leonardo mused that regardless of purdah
Killing the babies of animals was murder

Leonardo was wise in deed and word
All he needed was his word to be heard
While his ideas on air have taken flight
On that score Leo was also right so right

The Missionary and the Cannibal

Dave explained 'I eat fish and chicken'
And told us 'it's middle-class hypocrisy'
Making the finger-lickin' action

A perfect reason with no moral distraction
Dave is hardly a hypocrite
As it is only a little bit
Much like the Founding Fathers
Who declared as their prequel
'A self-evident truth all men are created equal'
Then proved it was a lie as there was no sequel
They meant all white American men
Who did not include anyone defined
As black or Indian or otherwise
So judges closed their prejudicial eyes
A fact that found support in the courts
Who declared with such an ease
Like a roe deer running wild
Were people they classed as Chinese

As for women well they should stay in the kitchen
Where they keep busy plucking a chicken
Or the bedroom where they can perhaps be picked
By a Wienstein-type with the feeling of criminals
For all women that the law has for all animals

The lesson Dave wants us to learn
Borne of his own values
As he is no kind of squit
Means he too must earn
And not seek to hide behind

A self-imposed label of hypocrite
It is a pale excuse as he taps his nose
That cannot stand scrutiny as he knows
Trying to pass it off only shows
A weak-kneed 'I know I shouldn't but...'
It is no different however it is put
Rest assured it is the same for sure
As someone saying 'I love animals,
But I like eating them more'

Any which way you look at it
It comes back to the same track
Dave acts in the way he does
Because he can
Because he is a man
Because an animal is a brand
It is grand to eat their flesh
And it salivates with the mesh
That drools from his lips and gathers
On his hips so the oil on his fingertips
Is not just gravy
But mixed in the bud with their blood

Dress up reason as a half-hearted excuse
So they remain under our thumbscrew
Because the belief of people like Dave
Makes the killing a choice
Not between two evils
But no evil at all:
For to kill someone alive is the choice
Made easier because that someone
Is a legal thing with no legal voice
In being a hypocrite

Rather than a hero or mentor we can see
Attenborough is perhaps like you and me
Much as the cannibals saw the missionaries
And almost started to believe
The sermons the Christians delivered
They eagerly were willing to receive
Yet when their belief was tested
They believed food was too good to waste
So the missionaries were boiled alive
Human lobsters with an even better taste

The problem is when you are hailed
As the most trusted man on the planet
You cannot afford to be seen
As one who acts as one more gannet
The danger is instead of one to inspire
You can be one whose tongue is on fire
Everything takes second-place to our desire
By those who parade lies as a password
Will steal your ideas as a thief of fire
Then use them as the currency of a liar
So animals dic while they quietly conspire

The Octopus Met Sisyphus

Though few clung to the sharp deal
Not knowing which one was unreal
As white is black and black is white
Faded in a freezing pettifog night
Out of mind as well as out of sight
Deaf to their cries beneath the waves
Their home became a watery trave
Eight arms bobbing as a lifeless cork
Once as alive as a harpooned orca
The crooked compass for the octopus
Pointing from east unto the West by us
Her corpus plight dark yet so luminous
Fish of every kind the wide ocean binds
Closed eyes that opened our minds
To the sight we are compelled to see
Mile on watery mile of a sad cemetery
Seeing a diseased sea of animal misery

The sailors sing a shanty lullaby
While a whole world fiddles faster
Than a looming out of tune Nero
Witnessing our blooming disaster
Spies the last octopus at minus zero
When her three hearts that remain
Are broken in time all the same

All that is left from the total sum
Is our theft in an ocean of scum
As the Chinese schooners circled
Then they hacked her eight arms off
A void on the ocean's telling schroff

The mountain sunk in a seasick scrum
Hidden by the drunken sailors' rum
The throttle of so many empty bottles
Mean we can only see a plastic sea
While we stumble mumble and gurgle
All the ocean's occupants are burgled
All we can see through bloodshot sighs
All we can see is our dross demolition
When the waves drown we can protest
Then sound off for a senseless abolition
As if it was by some oceanic revolution
Rather than death a calculated destitution

Forever rolling towards our pus
Minus outweighs a plus for us
Caught by the tentacles of truth
When we ask 'where is the body'
Then try to deny our focused eye
Faint-hearted and pusillanimous
When there is no habeas corpus
Reneged on our promise to protect
Now the octopus has met Sisyphus

The Palace of Plunder Land

Using a strange sign language he asked
'What have I done to deserve such a fate?'
As another inmate lined up
When the tiger opened the gate

Then the next in line asked
'Why am I locked inside this cage?'
As she was assigned her task
Flying in a circling swooping rage

And then the next and the next
Engaged in a weird pretext
All were lost in a pointless quest
Asking, 'Why pray are we here?
Are we to be perpetual deportees
Or shown dignity due to any guest'

For them there was no answer except
The one they could not bear to hear:
Each of you is our perpetual slave
We decide the time for your grave
For who is the jack and who is the knave
Has no meaning now you are in our power
Get used to the shock of your status as a slave
Now your world is ours every hour-on-hour

You will have to get used to the scene
You have an inside view of a human zoo
You have the picture that makes us richer
You are the prized part of our barbecue

The Pangolin's Saviour

Who cares if it is one more pangolin
Caught by a slice of the poacher's machete
Catching each scale with skin on skin
Dirty hands and sour heart so hot and sweaty

Who cares about one more pangolin
Killed in the rush of the poacher's crush
For the prize of their scales as medicine
Then left to die in agony alone in the bush

Who cares if it is one more pangolin
The most poached mammal on earth
It is hardly a crime or even a sin
Catching a creature for cash shows its worth

Who cares if it is one more pangolin
If it satisfies our never-ending vanity
Destined for the bin we rescued our kin
If not imagine what their fate would be

If we failed to rescue them
Think about their destiny
Dying in the wild in nature's misery
Far from being questionable behaviour
We are doing them all a favour
In killing them we are their saviour

They have been here 65 million years
There is no reason for crocodile tears
Living on our peopled planet
We are hardly a gannet

By eating their fleshy meat
Their scales as our medicine
Their blood as an aphrodisiac
Is hardly the act of an ego-maniac

The Phantom Vivisector

They strapped her in the cage
Bound her to the cold steel bars
Committed every scientific outrage
That they could gauge as both engaged
Injecting her arms and legs and chest
Into her head and brain and the rest
Then they injected poison in her eyes
When they were both bloodshot
They removed them in the time-slot

So they focused on the clock
By taking all her body apart
Leaving nothing intact except her heart
As they noted the data statistics
Part curiosity and wholly egotistic
When they finished stripping her bones
So she was just a blind skeleton
Their repeated experiment ended
When they swiftly killed their exhibit

The sabs broke into the secret lab
Balaclava clad in black vigilantes
And kidnapped the vivisectionist
To let him visit the circle of Dante
They prodded and probed his body
Then tracked the terrain of his insides
To trace what was there besides
The skill he had as a vivisector
As science's natural benefactor

They searched his body again
Up and down and down and up
With no regard to his pain
Though their search was in vain
To make sure they did everything
They even searched for his soul
Nevertheless they could never guess
The one organ they could not kick-start
They tried and failed to find his heart

They were flummoxed because it was
A conclusion they found hard to resist
Despite the instruments and scalpel minds
The sabs came to a confused conclusion
That proved to be a twist upon a twist
They failed to add his heart to their list
Though there was no reason to panic
For the absence was purely organic

Far from being an existential quest
They were defeated by truth's tempest
It was not something they had missed
What the sabs were seeking did not exist

The Price of a Pangolin

May you find that your scales
Will weigh in the seat of justice
Each one being a winding trail
Balanced against our Judas kiss

What is wrong with the pangolin
That we cannot take them in
Much as when the world began
We claim it was solely for man

For wherever we live
For them our world
Is where they are hurled
So our lives can pan out as planned
One more Wuhan is where we stand

For then with the pangolin's death
We can all breathe easily
Each has taken their last breath
For all in our world to see

Or is it the unjust impostor
That is visible in all of us
We stalk the jungle as a mass killer
Devoid of any feeling and no fuss

What is special about the pangolin
That we cannot use its skin
When their death gives us breath
Our best defence to a cruel coincidence
Their scales pales into insignificance

Balanced against being our medicine
The price of their life
Balanced against our need for sex
Is outweighed in so many ways
Sucked and swallowed by our vortex

Since 2000 a million have been massacred
They are the world's most traffic wild animal
Yet the world wants to ban friendly poachers
When it is only one more to trap and trammel
Your wish for to live a long life
Reflect the truth on your tongue
So you can roll in your jack-knife
To stay strong and mighty young
Then to wander in the wild
As you have always done
Avoiding the heads so defiled
Spend your days in the setting sun
May you find a peace you deserve
Then breathe in free and fine air
Keep your centre on the curve
Though in a world that does not care
You will only prise from our vice
What you need to be freed
From our dream and your nightmare
By the scales of law and a real prayer

The Question

I feel that animals are as bewildered as we
except that they have no words for it.
I would say that all life is asking:
"What am I doing here?"

Isaac Bashevis Singer

As with a terminal cancer
When there is no answer
Yet death has its own story
For we seek a sort of glory
Killing other creatures as a whim
A cull and profit our pseudonym
Even if gain is our holy wine hymn
Our autosuggestion denying rights
Demand for ourselves alone
Cuts others beyond the bone
Yet is wrong and can never be right
Asking, 'What am I doing here?'
Rest assured they are sure
They were not born to be forlorn
Or to be a perennial human thorn

Why do you figure you are blessed using a word
It could be nature's curse you have not heard
Stealing their song is not what kills the songbird

Our trump cards on the table
The supposed soul we borrow
From a self-ordained religion
Is only a ploy by us to avoid

Asking the ultimate question
We share with a polar bear
Plus every raggedy pigeon
A corpse of truth laid bare
Sitting on our judgement chair
A natural bias naturally unfair
An arrow of lies we can never retract
An epitaph proving our ego is intact
On our shadowed idea we sell as a fact
Living a lie trips easily off each tongue

Hidden as an ambitious politician's bung
Using our falsehood deeds undercover
To conceal so others do not discover
Though we know it is pure sophistry
Burning trials and witches against her
A passé-partout we pretend is true
We alone are a nation of animal lovers

The Seal of a Suffragette

Gertrude Ansell took up the cudgel
For those held under the thumb
By those who had become
Masters at the table dropping breadcrumbs
Holders of the key and masters of the fate
Keeping animals and women outside the gate
Except when awaiting their fate inside the gate
Of the man-made prison to be force-fed to death
Of a vivisection lab for a science shibboleth

Mary Clarke was the mistress of protest
Who smashed the State's secret armour
She figured that was meant to harm her
And the women and animals too
As she flew into their political nest
As ever as an unwanted guest
Full of life and too much zest
Yet she was bound to lose the contest
When the guards placed her under arrest

They lined her up and held her down
Her arms and legs strapped tight
Forced her neck to catch the light
Forced her head to hang up right
Her body primed so she could swallow
Her mind ready for their kind of gallows
To them she was just another dogsbody
Then they poured the food inside her body
Just another busybody who was nobody
Who counted for nothing with anybody
They filled the tube right to the brim

And poured and poured every last drop
So nothing was wasted as their grip
Held her neck as tight as a noose
They needed no excuse for their abuse
When Mary Clarke became a human goose

Mary was one more suffragette
They would choose to soon forget
Strike her down without any regret
When the water and the gruel was fed
By force to destroy her liver and head
Poured and poured until they were sure
Mary was deader than a Dodo is dead

The Serial Culler

The empty promise full of bull
Formed from a matching mind
Of false ideals as truth gone blind
Lost in a way they will never find
It counts for little as another lull
All it adds up to is another cull

The numbers are too many
So we have to find a way
To get rid of the past and the pest
That threatens to eat our hay
And eat into our profits and sales
Run them off our land with rails
A speeding shot will silence their wails

Who can object when the victim
Cannot avoid what will hit him
While our only motive is money
That jangles as we talk and walk
Send them to their deaths in cages
As our pellets of poison rages
Through their open veins
In the end all that remains
Will be a mounting mountain heap
Of the red and the dead six feet deep

With souls emptier than a broken drum
Our pockets jingle and our profits hum
As another bound silent victim
Whose lifeline grows forever dim
Caught in the cross-hair cull

As she lines up to take her turn
The target for the marksman's yearn
Spins out of control as the deed is done
To deny her another day in the sun
When as killer and culler
Our lives are much fuller
When we proudly become one

The Spin We Are In

Although we know your aim
Is to avoid our gassy methane
We are not to blame
As at heart all we do
Is the same act as you
Belch and burp as digestion starts
Then ends when we like you too
Stand and deliver thunderous tarts
Do not deceive us
When all the fuss
Is over for yourself
We are not on your shelf
All that will be left of us
Will be more stale pus

The world will still spin
Without you and me in it
The world will still spin
Each climate change minute
The world will still spin
When you forget who saves
You from sinking below waves
The world will still spin
When you are on your knees
Praying to us birds and bees

The world will still spin
When we share secrets
With the grass and trees
The world will still spin
When icebergs drown your land

334

A polar bear cries on faded sand
A polar bear dies on poisoned sand

The world will still spin
When sun parches your plans
Yet who among you has a clue
Whether a sea is brown or blue
The world will still spin
If we are blind in each eye
If we fail to even see the sky
The world will still spin
Out of control devoid of spirit and soul
Disappearing time's hand cannot be held
Falling fast as our failure is self-propelled
Spinning towards our desolate infinity
As the last human is stung by the last bee

The Story of the Last Slave Barracoon

The Clotilda sailed in 1859
Long after the crossed legal line
Abolishing all the imported slaves
When Timothy Meaher placed a bet
That he could easily defy the law
Using a cargo of slaves as a debt

Meaher owned a lot of people
All black and bruised and blue
He kept as human specimens
Confined in chains and pens
Proud of his natural historic flaw
Yet prouder he would defy the law

Meaher boasted about his bullion
He saw people's deaths as a steeple
For his bullion made him millions
Their lives a one-way ride to oblivion
Glad as a Chad-type to deny the law
Bragging how he alone defied the law

Captain Foster risked their lives
Accepting the bet rounded up 110
Black children and women and men
As the gamblers breached the law
Huddled close in their chained place
Making sardines seem well-spaced

Foster knew the penalty for his enterprise
He would be hanged before public eyes
His mind fixed firm on defying the law

He saw slaves as a personal cat's-paw
Foster swaggered aboard with braggadocio
Foster figured he truly sailed above the law

The lure of the one-eyed bounty
Was too great for him to care
Foster delivered Meaher's gold
Keeping slaves 45 days in the cold
Darkness of the cramped damp hold
While the children clamped in chains
Cried out day and night for their Mama
He shed his cargo on a shore in Alabama
Boasting of how easily he broke the law
Coasting and toasting all that he saw
Captured in chains for caveat emptor
Crowing as their owner and tormentor

The Clotilda laid on a river bed in Mobile
Deep below where the slaves were delivered
Any surviving slaves who did not die
Were checked by Meaher's naked eye

Meaher and Foster were proud of the lacuna
They found with *The Clotilda* as a schooner
The last ship bringing slaves to America
As plantation fodder for Uncle Tom's cotton
Meaher talked about people and creatures
When the loud shout from a local preacher
Matched the flag-flying ever-rebel teacher
With false pride having defied the law
With their cargo of human scrimshaw

Yet the brave revolutionary Redoshi
Started the settlement of Africatown
Rejected the crass cloaked cult clowns
Intent on bringing all of them down
Where they escaped to chase liberty
To forge their brand of being free
Yet Meaher tried hard to win his bet
Denying survivors the right to be free
The rest sunk in their rusty chains
Clanking in the murky Mobile quay

Yet the worst of the tale
Was told by Cudge Lewis
Who was dying of thirst on *The Clotilda*
When the Captain on orders from Meaher
When the shackled merchandise
Had safely crossed the border
Revealed that the food and drink
Denied to them by his hoodwink
Was for the animals pulling his plough
So they were fattened here and now
The American free spirit at play
Echoing a claimed Independence Day
Slaves should be glad some survived
On the food left over by the animals
For Meaher and Foster the cargo was incidental
Meaher and Foster were proud pioneer criminals
Seeing and selling slaves ranked below animals
Reflecting the Native American law
Riddled with flaw-upon-flaw
Trading truth for falsehood

Lies growing forever obese
Like every judge of Cochise
Like every judge stealing land
From the Apaches and Choctaw
Using a bent cast-iron biased law
Meeting and cheating their peers
Drowned them in a Trail of Tears
A prejudiced judge in the *Dred Scott Case*
Upholding racism with a crude Klan face
Proving impure American Law as a disgrace

In 2022 they raised remains of *The Clotilda*
Seeing the chains and shackles in the dust
Black limbs between iron branded in rust
Yet for a bet slaves were buried in mud
Their lifelines traced by percolated blood
You wonder about Foster and Meaher's epitaph
Perhaps 'Here lie two slavers who made a living
Drowning men women and children in a flood
Of force-filled-fear to surrender their lifeblood'
But swamped in the darkest deepest water
Foster and Meaher saw slaves as a cargo
Much as animals in one of our abattoirs
As with our demands for more and more
With abuse as a repertoire and an encore

They won a bet by stealing lives
From those too weak to survive
Sending the slaves to their graves
Covering up by destroying the evidence
Escaping prosecution for their evil birth
Yet justice reaches way beyond this earth
A salutary lesson for all such criminals

Justice survives way beyond any water slaughter
Justice sees through the eyes of animals and slaves
Justice drowns everything with its defeating waves
Justice is truth in action that speaks from the grave

The 21st Century Treblinka

Do you hate the Nazis
With their cruel passion
Do you hate the Nazis
Devoid of all compassion

Do you hate the Nazis
Whose abuse has no ration
Do you hate the Nazis
Seeing victims cold and ashen

Then both near and far
Think about their mirror
Whether or not in uniform
It was shaped and deformed
On their creed of cruelty
Whether far or near
Reflected in their mirror
Whether far or near
It was their chance to preen
On a face each must have seen

Do you hate the Nazis
Whose instinct was to kill
Do you hate the Nazis
Destroying each stranger's will

Do you hate the Nazis
Ovens they intended to fill
Do you hate the Nazis
Murder their practised skill

Do you hate the Nazis
Who were common criminals
Do you hate the Nazis
Valued people below animals

It made Isaac Singer see the sight
And hear the woeful sound
Of their frightened flight
And their hearts start to pound
Nostrils twitching at an awful smell
Only the toughest victim could tell
Then delivered the eternal stinker
That damned every clinker
Damned every head shrinker
The truth on removing his blinker
Made Isaac a prophet and a thinker:
To animals we are all Nazi's
And for them it's an eternal Treblinka

Cattle packed like sardines in cattle trucks
Lined up in a clanking chained queue
Among the remains of their stomachs
Splashing through the mud and muck
Prodded and stunned by electric guns
Bleeding from every forced orifice
Bleeding from fear while speechless
We all choose to forget our trespass
Only remembering what we tasted before
So our open palate and closed heart
Clamours for more and more and more

Our modern concentration camp
Is a version of a new Ravensbruck

342

Our modern factory farm
Is designed purely to harm
The inmates that enter the gates
For whom only torture awaits
No one cares and no one grieves
No one who enters ever leaves
Crowded closer than herrings in a tin
Caught between a crime and a sin
Line-by-line with no escape from fate
Our daily dose of animal morphine
Our factory farm starts with a cow
Or a lamb or a pig or a sheep
Whose bits and giblets we reap
Replacing a feigned culture with torture
While our victims thrash and die in a heap

Are the English and Faroese and Japanese
Mere doppelgangers of the Germans
Seeing them as the same species
No different to the others you see
Especially those we foster
Particularly those impostors
Whose masks hide you from me
Morally we know we are pygmies
For animals we are all Nazis
A factory farm our jackboot arm
A creation for those creatures
Their death our favourite feature
All we learn from those teachers
While living in our glitzy global Ritz
As their body shatters and mind splits
In our world as an Animals' Auschwitz

The Virus of love Revisited

Down so low I could not see what was up
You held my splintered soul in your heart's cup
Reached my waving hand with a wounded paw
Leading me on the ladder of love's law

There were times that I was not strong enough
When I buckled as the road was too rough
You rescued me with tough words straight and true
Now if I roam all roads lead back to you

I feel as free as wild bees in the trees
Pleased to be caught by your love-bird disease
Freed by the fever of your luck-filled love
Locked and lost in the virus of your love

I fought the lonely 3 a.m. feeling
Fixed on the only one my heart thought of
My mind was mixed up and rocked and reeling
Calmed by your touch as tender as a velvet glove
Though through that long night
I was filled with lonely fright
My lonesome spirit was askew and still raging
My mind was rambling and my body was ageing
You proved the one contagion worth catching
Is the flame-filled virus of love

You may not know the language
You may not know the words
You may not know my name
Yet as a lifeline giver what you delivered
As the last arrow in your love's quiver
Saved me and is strictly not for the birds

Time-bomb Heart

It's a beautiful day
Let's go out and destroy something

There's a blood-red sky kissed by a passing wispy cloud
Blood on the lips of the circling hungry vulture crowd
Death on the teeth of the unleashed invading hound
Blood in the bubble that traps her pleading crying voice
Death on the blade that destroys his future crushed choice
Blood on her forehead is the child's forever losing prize
Death on our hands after the first Kremlin bullet flies
Blood in the mind of the Russki's manufactured lies
Death on the tongue of Putin while he tries to paralyse
Blood on the sword of Islam serving to cannibalise
Death in the word of the Taliban seeking to terrorise
Matching the fear-filled light doused in freedom's dying
eyes

It's a beautiful day
Let's go out and murder truth

Too Much Monkey Business

The Chinese Academy of Sciences
Now use all their advanced appliances
For a fantastic project to make monkeys fat
To make more money for a shareholder bull
Progress to move from a monkey to a fat cat
Feeding them with way too much food
So all their organs began to expand
Soon they all needed a gastric band
Obviously a band was denied to them
As the project proved making them slim
The progress of their unhealthy whim
By manufacturing a pill making them obese
Manufacturing a pill making their heart cease
Then they suffer by a massive metabolic rate
Changing from being very fat to very thin
When their bodies are blown up then shrunk
From an obese hunk to a malnourished monk
A Chinese scientist blessed by being obese
So engrossed took part in the experiment
Taking pill after pill and tablet after tablet
With a surfeit of the multi- coloured drugs
The same as he had fed to the monkeys
In no time he too became mega-obese
Taking his participation to the limit
On the path of the monkey's progress
He too lost so much weight he moved
From mere emancipation to total emaciation
Until too late he realised that an experiment
For the monkeys finished in a no-win final
When he keeled over and joined a triangle pile
To be incinerated as part of the useless data

That he intended to send to pretend to use later
Seeing the frozen startled eyes of the monkeys
As the by-products of an obese disease
Caused by him as a misguided scientist
Like him they had lost too much weight
Leaving his own lesson way too late
Before the information could be filed
Like them he was one more on the pile
From the seat of being forced to be obese
A date with an experimental fate
Locked in his own scientific end
With only zero around the bend
A cascade of carcasses on the rack
Joined by one now pinprick thin
The last of those recently deceased
Proof truth is neither white nor black

Toxic Soup in the Tide

The spilled sewage flowed free
From factory to river to the sea
Hour-after-hour week-by-week all year long
No one caring whether it was right or wrong
The mass polluters were well known
Here and there and everywhere
They were or happen to roam

The sewage flows in a soupy loop
Chemicals of all forms in the group
Water turns colour with no solution
Fish farmed disease an unnatural evolution
From factory to fish to cancer as our coup
A story to ignore as no one wants our scoop
As we await a self-created virus revolution

We can sup with the dictator devil
Using a long Putin table and rusty spoon
Knowing it will never be on the level
There is no guide for a freedom ride
If we decide to sup with a tainted spoon
Our toxic soup washes up in every tide
Until the time beckons us all too soon

Eyes still fail to see past evil swill
That serves to shine but exists to kill
Hiding the beauty of an invisible moon
Although we already know a toxic truth
There is no one among us ever immune
As we willingly sip the poisoned soup
With our own spiked Putin spoon

Tulsa Massacre Anniversary 1921-2021

In June 1921 the rednecks led the mob
Against the blameless black community
Based and built on a blatant lie
They saw their opportunity
To use Jim Crow law
To demolish the buildings and churches
And homes and murder 300 black people
On their bent principles and crooked steeple
In a veiled genocide

Yet the rednecks of Tulsa
Wore their badge of dishonour
With a perverted pride
Having razed the hospital to the ground
They sought to raze their hate from history
By making their massacre a mystery

Nevertheless truth can never be hidden
Whatever the De La Beckwiths of the world
Figure when their life flag is unfurled

In two days they murdered 300 people
10,000 men and women and children
Were rendered homeless by their unity
Of redneck prejudice and purpose
To destroy the complete community
By arson and looting and lynching
They tried to hang Dick Rowland
For no reason save being black
And everyone on the wrong side
Of the redneck racist Tulsa track

Burgling the home of an 80-year-old man
Paralysed and too crippled to walk
His wife begged for his life
A witness says 'the damn dogs shot him'
Then they torched his home
For good measure they murdered his wife

Then they found a black blind man
With no legs who moved on wheels
The mob roped him like a steer
Tied him to the back of a truck
And laughed as they pulled him
Up and down Main Street
As he squealed like a stuck pig
They revved with even greater zeal
Firing the night with an executioner's seal
He died beneath their spinning wheels

Then they found Andrew Cheesten Jackson
The surgeon held his hands up in surrender
Instead the committed cold-blooded murder
Cut down by two trigger-happy white offenders
Though he pleaded for his life
Their bullets took their toll
Bleeding to death before their eyes
While they saw his murder as their prize
He could not be saved in the only hospital
That served the black people all around
Caught in their hate-filled bubble
The hospital was just a pile of rubble
The mob had burned it to the ground

Yet who were the rednecks
And who was not is easy to check
Like the German citizens and the Nazi's
The Tulsa cops and the owners of shops
The businessmen and the mayor
Were all part of the play and players
Even the judge could not be fussed to budge
Instead they wiped the memory of the dead
From the history of their story and warped glory
Because they knew that every man
Who murdered the 300 guiltless black people
Were or sided with the guilt-riddled Klan

A hundred years later
Though the Tulsa authorities
Tried to bury the truth
Not realising no one can escape
From its natural superiority

A group of mourners gathered around
Some felt a magnetic pull
They dug where they stood
And found mass graves of those
Who were buried in the clothes
They died in when the murderous
Tulsa redneck citizens were barbarous
Their deeds were discovered
As truth always is regardless of the clutches
For despite their desperate attempts to hide
Their deeds could never be concealed
When their attempt at ethnic genocide
Of people holding the bones of their pets
Spoke with the earthquake of death

The victims' magnetic voice revealed
Nothing could hide the multiple-murder
That all the skeletons concealed

What was doomed to fail as every dog knows
When he buries a bone however far from home
The grave never forgets however deep the ruth
The taste on his wisdom tooth
Will never be strong enough to bury truth

Until the cows do not come Home

Some people see a cow as sacred
See something within their form
Making them somehow special
Turning them into a kind of deiform

Yet he saw each cow as ugly
Saw something within their form
That made each one uglier than him
Using it as a disguise to misinform

He called the politician 'a fat cow'
Saw something in their rotund form
Making them as useful and useless
As a politician with a brainstorm

The rapist called his victim a cow
Learning to use their huge form
As abuse from a woman to an animal
His guilt as a transferred platform

Their sleazy words of hate as split silk
Shows their boast has a value of their ilk
They do not know you cannot kill the cow
Then quench a thirst by drinking their milk

Voyage of *The Zong*

In 1781 Captain Luke Collingwood
Claimed he had no choice
He had to rely on his inner voice
His cargo was in danger
He had to protect the property
As the content was somewhat stranger
So they tried hard to hide
By using a kind of embargo
By chance Olandah Equino discovered
The content of the overloaded cargo

Claiming they were running out of water
His choice was between making a profit
And losing the money he would forfeit
He had to decide who counted for squit

The ship was laden with so many slaves
There was no easy answer as to who to save
Because the decision counted for more than
Some children and women and so many
shackled black men

One-by-one the sailors threw the slaves
Into the deep merciless stormy waves
Day-after-day for three full days
Collingwood ordered the sailors
To throw the men women and children
To their chained water-filled graves
Until 133 slaves sank beneath the waves

The case of the slaves was sheer despair
As the chains dragged them down
Far below the unforgiving sea
Their deaths as certain as a slaves' misery
Their cries drowned as they were too
At the bottom of the ocean red and blue

The case involved more than bees and honey
It revolved around a claim for insurance money
So the decision had to be one that would convince
A tough Judge whose knowledge was never runny

Lord Mansfield weighed each term of the contract
He balanced what mattered in loss and gain
His judgment was nothing to do with the impact
He was not judging the deaths or even pain
His only concern was to follow the money train
Then what *The Zong Case* finally decided
When Mansfield followed the legal course
Of judging the farrago of the unwanted cargo
The value of a slave was half that of a horse

Granville Sharp tried in vain
To name and try the murderous crew
But as it was only a cash-valued cargo
The law defeated what he sought to do
Collingwood escaped his earthly justice
Though he had an almighty price to pay
Like the 133 slaves he murdered
Fate captured the seafarer torturer
For before he could be tried
He joined that cargo no-return journey
While on terra firma he collapsed and died
Finally facing his own judgement day

We Can See the Sea

The whale is already fetid
Her tail as rancid and stale
As a politician's promise to be honest
As the impossible is hard to achieve
Once we had a reason to believe
Now somehow fading away we see
While more cling to a sweet ideal
The left and right day and night
Will be alright
As long as we can see the sea

The shark has lost his fins
His tail as rancid and stale
As a predator's promise to shed malice
For a future only a seer could foresee
The daytime darkness raises a plea
Forcing us to realise but still see
While more cling to a sweet ideal
The left and right day and night
Will be alright
As long as we can see the sea

Seals have shed their mottled skin
As if they were pleading volunteers
Neither seeking to resist or prohibit
Ocean research by a Japanese scientist
When anyone asks about anything
Of anyone any time of day you see
While more cling to a sweet ideal
The left and right day and night

Will be alright
As long as we can see the sea

The alligator has snapped his chain
Hose-washed blood erased his name
Along with our memory and his pain
As the claim for a stylish handbag
Is our sole promise that now remain
A search-party sold his life we see
While more cling to a sweet ideal
The left and right day and night
Will be alright
As long as we can see the sea

The crocodile has lost her smile
Drowned in her own forced tears
A blunt knife pierces her wary eye
Seasick sailors search for a lullaby
When she lost her life in sheer fear
Her body pulled by the boat you see
While more cling to a sweet ideal
The left and right day and night
Will be alright
As long as we can see the sea

Dolphin numbers have shrunk
Most lost in a sky blue funk
The scale of the tale they can tell
A stench of a rigour mortis smell
Time for us and them is long gone
Reflecting on our passing we see
While more cling to a sweet ideal
The left and right day and night

Will be alright
As long as we can see the sea

Lobsters changed from pink to black
After a maven armed Spanish attack
Halted breath with limbs idly hacked
The sailors played on any living prey
Passing time towards a judgement day
So there was no way back you see
While more cling to a sweet ideal
The left and right day and night
Will be alright
As long as we can see the sea

Oysters lost their survival shell
When they were all pulverised
By forces from a man-made hell
No rocking at the base of the sea
They grew respected and protected
Until we stole their home you see
While more cling to a sweet ideal
The left and right day and night
Will be alright
As long as we can see the sea

All we can see is the bed of the sea
A rust-riddled floor barely visible
A bed stripped bare yet indivisible
No water now no water anywhere
Salt has turned brooding and dark
The seal has somehow lost her bark
A stark mark hidden from you and me
Blind as we are to our guiding star

For what we see is what we cannot see
We are what we figured we would never be
The land has lost her last torched tree
The sky cries her sad secret silence
For the last uncaged blue-bird
For the free lonely spoiled sea
Kissed by the lonesome land
Reaching out for any true hand
From the sparked lightning stars
Locked behind our human bars
While all the waters burn
Frames our failure to learn
A lesson lifeline of our lifetime
As the last dolphin sighs then dies
Before her intended rightful time

A drooped head of a dying swan
Found a bed she never wanted
Seeped in pools of spreading red
A sleep of the long-time dead
Yet the cataracts of our poison
Tethered to the end of our rope
We face figures we cannot see
Even with a magnified telescope
Less than abandon a sweet ideal
There is a loss of our hope you see
The left and right day and night
Will never be alright
It is not in our sight
For now it can never be

We only listen to self-serving alibis
As a shuttered camera snaps our lies

Willing to be blinded by blurred eyes
We have no need of a clairvoyant
When we can still be nonchalant
Our future forged on a sour spree
A fog-brained present for you and me
We see a fogged future for you and me
The periscope's view is now destroyed
Without any dressed-up excuse or ploy
There is no reason we can be buoyed
Now we can no longer see the sea

What Am I Bid

Without Elvis it was still Jailhouse Rock
While linked chains clinked out of time
To the Blues tune No More Auction Block
Abandoned hope of all past their prime
With justice on trial in the market dock
English Law ticks out our foxed false clock

The men inspected the goods
No one wanted to buy the duds
They felt their legs and rump
They figured some could jump
Others would make a good pump
If they will all avoid any trump
Though some were far too fat
Yet leaner were meaner at that
They wanted one who would
Accept the role of a new stud
They had no use for some crud
Or any disease that was in bud
They checked their age and eyes
Making sure there were no dyes
The farmers would use any ruse
To sell their goods at auction
Trading for a heavy puncheon

Whether it was a machine or a tractor
Was just one more pornographic factor
All the seller cared about was the price
All that was on their head without lice
For this time as last and next time
The goods had to be in their prime

The deal done so the owner thrived
Sailed in the business of selling lives
An auction block selling substitute cattle
The beauty of war without any battle
The men counted the pieces of silver
Walked away with a head full of knives
Glad of the feeling the free money drives
For the dumping of the abandoned items
By ugly double-chinned pot-bellied men
Bullying drunkard philandering husbands
Whose vainglory keeps their ego trip alive
An auction with men selling unwanted wives

What Colour is an Animal

Some are black some are white
Some are a symbol you can believe
Knowing to grieve is just alright
For on the darkest of dark nights
The only one with visionary eyes
Is the one we have come across
Figured she was an inedible criss-cross
So worthy only of our double-cross
Hammer bullets harder than steel nails
Through the chest of the broken-winged
Creature so free she is beyond being ringed
Yet we force a gloss on the tarnished dross
Creating our topos of a crooked constant chaos
A future lost for us when failing to see
Our murder of the glaze-eyed albatross

Some are sun some are rain
Some are a storm warning omen
Following the Roman still in pain
Tracked without reason to hide or feign
Fixed and focused with cloudless eyes
Failing to realise the two-headed toss
Is no answer to the blood-filled pail
Holding the remains of death's cold sting
A creature so free she is beyond being ringed
Through the chest of the broken-winged
Yet we force a gloss on the tarnished dross
Creating our topos of a crooked constant chaos
A future lost for us when failing to see
Our murder of the glaze-eyed albatross

There is no truth to prove
When we boldly seek to lose
The label of a certain killer
Choosing bathos to replace ethos
A blast furnace heart of Nazi asbestos
Lies are more than a mere double-cross
When we pilloried the saddled albatross

The albatross can be spied
The albatross can be fried
The albatross can be vilified

There is no truth to prove
When we boldly seek to lose
Lies are more than a mere double-cross
When we pilloried the saddled albatross
For there is more than one biased view
That neither the confused priest or you
Can see whether you are far or near
Unlike the albatross who lives and looks
From the other side of the refracted mirror

The albatross has survived
The albatross has thrived
The albatross has arrived
The albatross was alive
The albatross was deprived
The albatross was sky rived
The arrow in each claw and wing
The agony of law no voice can sing
The albatross soar has been denied
The albatross augury is now defied
Hanging as the ghost of justice cried

Nailed in a scarlet cloudless sky dive
Suspended with her wide wings extended
Her fate and fortune and future forever
A miscarriage of justice by our fixed conviction
Lost to our cost we are stricken by her crucifixion

White is right about being Black

Martha was always the one
Who knew from the start
That she had to ignite
The fire inside her heart
When she was dog-tired
And tired of being treated like a dog
Not allowed to sit down on a bus
And addressed as if she was a hog
She knew it was time for action
Against the racist bus company
No time for her to pettifog
Against their Jim Crow sanctimony
Just because she was black
No reason to be ill-treated
Martha sat down on the only free seat
Reserved only for one who was white
Martha cared not a jot
She knew what was wrong
She sure as hell knew what was right
Martha planted her feet
Firmly on the ground
Then sat down on the seat
She was harangued by the driver
He told her to move
Because she was black
Martha was a sole survivor
She knew this was the time
It was not time to turn back
Her chance to take a stance
Grab this opportunity
To demand her share of dignity

Proving she was on the right track
Showing the world she was black
So when they called the police
Martha sat down to stand up
Against their racist caprice
She was no longer willing
To be treated like an animal
She was burned out
By the whipping and lynching
As if she was a criminal
Or worse as if she was an animal
Martha knew it was time
To honour her ancestors
And her descendants
For her to make a stand against
Being confined and ring fenced
By the cheap cloaked creepy KKK
Who killed her kinsfolk every day
And made her feel second-class
As if she was some kind of ass
She could not let it pass
It was time for a volte-face
Martha ignited her light
And struck some sparks
That years later spread
Throughout the land
Turning America on its head
She inspired MLK
She inspired Rosa Parks
By lighting the darkness
Martha held the torch that scorched
The racists in and out of court
Yes rest assured she was the one

Who had the guts to start the fight
To prove what is wrong
To show it cannot be right
To deny them treating her
As an animal and a criminal
As if it was a sin to be born with black skin
She was fighting for her kin
So the little lady from Baton Rouge
Who set out once and for all to prove
Her desert and dignity was no different
Than any racist just because of her birth
Though their prejudice was rife
Cutting her heart like a jack-knife
She refused to buckle or bend
She fought to the bitter end
She showed them she was right
She proved that being black
Was no different than being white
She would not be their whipped dog
Like them she had no reason to cower
She was more than some racist's cog
That was her potency and lasting power
That is the lifetime legacy of Martha White

Who Breaks a Butterfly upon a Wheel

Who breaks a butterfly upon a wheel
Who among you could resist using power
To destroy some creature somewhere
For no reason except to know how it feels
Who would not find someone fragile
Then harm to induce a sly secret smile
Yes I guess we have to confess
Our power over the powerless
Captured by a never sated lust
As the archetypal man who is crushed
Where he is pushed around by his boss
Goes home to hit a woman as he is cross
Who then smacks her child for her loss
When he then kicks the sleeping pet cat
Followed by kicking a rusty crushed can
Without cause or reason other than
Using strength makes him feel like a man
Hurting someone weaker because you can
So it comes and so it goes
While second-rate Hirst art flows
A million wings broken while no one cries
Biased bars against a gaoled butterfly
Their hurt makes a coward feel real
On oh so many days
In oh so many ways
When what we condemn in other men
We practise on a sunflower stem
Spraying the harmless honey bees
Scorching the torched land and trees
Anywhere there is one more deal
Anytime there is one more life to steal

For all of us has an instant appeal
Compelled to purloin the last silent squeal
Inflicting a wound which will never heal
You need look no further than their ordeal
To see the effect of each weal
As our power is the final seal
A sound closer than the last chime peel
Hirst is not the first or the worst
Where the butterflies are broken
Without a word being spoken
Our wheels within wheels is a cloudburst
Hirst counts profits on his poverty graph
Killing a million butterflies as his epitaph
Confined in a truth that is all too real
As to who breaks a butterfly upon a wheel

Who sees the real You

Confucius said we should not do anything
To others that we would not do to ourselves
Though whether he said that after seeing
The bodies on the abattoir shelves
The bodies on the butchers' shelves
The bodies on the circus shelves
The bodies on the designer shelves
The bodies on the experimenters' shelves
The bodies on the freedom-fighters' shelves
The bodies on the gallows-birds' shelves
The bodies on the hook shop shelves
Without a fair-minded honest jury of twelve
That can analyse lies and continue to delve
Remains as unknown as his shrunken bones
Yet we know that unlike Pilate and Judas
The lesson worth the learning
Was the one lived by the noble Confucius

Why do You Love to Hate Me

If you are neutral in situations of injustice
You have chosen the side of the oppressor:

Desmond Tutu: *The Arch*

Why do you want to make my start in life an end
Why are you packing your abattoirs with my kind
Why are you a butcher without me on your mind
Why are you a hunter intent on ripping me apart
Why are you a carnivore content to gorge my heart
Why are you a scientist aiming to vivisect my soul
Why are you a rapist ready to destroy my whole
Why are you a farmer cramping me in your stall
Why are you caging me in your human zoo at all
Why are you a pornographer selling me as a toll
Why are you a jockey whipping my frightened foal
Why are you in a sordid sex saga so my life is spent
Why are you a pornographer with a sacrificial moll
Why are you crushing me for your pervert sense
Why are you a politician killing me by your con cull
Why are you stealing lives you deem void and null

When you face Camus' judgement day
What will you say about those you flay
What will you pray as our blood spurts away
What is your vision seeing us as your prey

Burn the blindness from my eyes and let me see
Burn the blindness from your eyes to let me be
Search my soul with your justifying line of lies
Then I too will know why you love to hate me

Wild Things We Think We Love You

In 2022 a herd of bison
Were being released
In the woods of Kent
To reintroduce the bison
Where their ancestors
Were exterminated by us
Only 6000 or so years ago
But now
We can forego their woe
Vaccinated with renewed passion
With no reason for us to be riled
For any of the species in the wild

Although it is not quite that simple
As bison kill the bark and eat trees
As the lynx before them with bees
Rub their thick fur against the trunk
Shifting where the bees lurk alive
A deadwood home for the woodpecker
While we can still fulfil our role
As a self-appointed countryside wrecker

The wild cats are alive again
Basking in sun drenched Scotland
Which is slightly odd as it is said
Domestic and wild cats are inter-bred
A peculiar species of a different kind
If the experiment is a success
Then they can live again in Devon
Safe from gun-toting poachers
On a short step to a rural heaven

Then again even if it fails
Our sterling ship still sails
We already have the past proof
Wild cats went through the roof
With a feeling of perverse pride
As before England will decide
To follow a prejudiced distinction
Then hunt them again to extinction

Long ago in the 18th century
The last white-tailed eagle
Flew through English skies
Disappeared as the last one died
At our hands throughout the land
Persecuted by us as perpetrators
We figured they harmed other birds
That was the root of their destruction
As we wanted to be the only ones
To kill the smaller birds for pleasure
After all what were bullets made for
Except our partial penchant for leisure
Except for our use in war and killing
Caught by us as the wild and willing
People and birds as sheer fun
For you and me and everyone
Except of course the dead eagle
Yet who cares when killing is legal

Now we intend to reintroduce
The supreme white-tailed eagle
In Scotland and the Isle of Wight
We have somehow seen the light
Much wiser to split the magpie miser

Then in time as is our constant way
When the new visitor has outstayed
Their welcome in crowded skies
They end up in crisp fresh pies
Use our bullets for a new war
What else are bullets made for
Except killing us plus other animals
As a rabbit is their rarebit
Each a ready-made target
Patiently awaiting a casket
Longing for a drooling retriever
To return with a heavy mouth
Then fill another empty basket

In the UK we have had no bears
For well in excess of 1000 years
Hence we had to be content
With a second-rate sense of bull-baiting
People denied their natural inclination
To draft stories about bears in the wood
Chain and train them to dance for us
As Elvis was a human dancing chicken
For Colonel Tom and his finger licking
Hot plate device that made them holler
Elvis and the chickens learned to dance
As the Colonel counted mounting dollars
Forget the squalor and dance in the parlour
Then when the dance is over
We can unlock their chains
As our new slave beyond their time
The song and dance rots at the stem
Surpassed by our need to kill them

With my bow and Arrow

It is such a bore
And a chore for some hairy boar
To have to be removed from the groove
Of the huertas which smell so sweet
And are even better to eat
So when the wild art creatures
Are denied food to live
When after all the huertas are ours
Taking hours to cultivate so your mouth
Has to go south
It is for the best that they all go west
As the hunters with a bow and arrow
So the point hits the vein
And all that remains is the rain
If the spattered black blood
And of course the unremitting pain
When the hunter fails in his aim
When he succeeds
The smell of blood
Causes the other boars to flee as to stay
Invites an arrow as they eat a marrow
And are despatched where they stand
Though hunting in England
By the bow is now banned
Because it is too cruel
So it is better it is used there
Where except for the bores in Parliament
The real ones are not shot where they stand
Content to hide outside the pain
As modern-day replicas of faked-eyed Petain

Equally it is little wonder such an enterprise
Is followed by a clown in camouflage
Who has the dazed mind and blank eyes
And a heart as cold as a Titanic iceberg
Appealing to the frozen soul of Zuckerberg
Seeking the truffle finding boar
As Zucker is a sucker for tucker
Maybe he will meet a man with a mirror

When Zucker meets his mucker
And tucks into his tucker
Hears the rhymes of changing times
When the death bell chimes
With no reason to fumble
As his loaded poised rifle
Moves from goat to pig to boar
He should stand close to the mirror
Then Zucker will instantly recognise
Which animal is the Pulitzer prize bore

Words will never hurt Me

She called her fast friend a pig
Because it was so sexist
Demeaned her with a chosen word
Showing how bias is kissed
Then dismissed her as a bitch
Because it was so sexist
Knowing that she had heard
Showed us she should not exist
She is too close to a modern witch
We condemned her in a cat fight
For being as sly as a wily fox
The slur digs deep and goes far
Into the ridges of her heart's radius
Where it challenges her mixed ethos
Hurting her as intended is obvious
So it promotes a natural prejudice
Knowing she heard the hatred of the herd
It hit the target of her heart
As was the aim of each tainted word

No need to philosophize
We can use hate as lies
Sticks and stones may well break bones
Yet words are the wounds we reap
Years later words still make us weep
Words stay as a loan we always own
Knowing every day we can never repay

Comparing her to any animal
Places her value as minimal
Making the hidden hurt subliminal

Using a curse to denounce her as worse
Than every average valueless animal
Strikes as hard as their blood seeps
For with a swish the wounded wish
Reserved for them on a scrapheap
Condemning BLM while denying ALM
Forever cuts and hurts her scalpel deep

Written in Water

Burn the blue moon so it cries in the sky
Sell our soul while the whole world starts to fry
Chase the last polar bear with blood-lust eyes
Our false valentine of death in disguise

The stream dries and dies before our eyes
Poisoned by all our phoney leaders' lies
Our world plunges towards destiny's cell
For this time the chime strikes our own death knell

Icebergs melt on the horizon
When the heat keeps on rising
The polar bear is caught in our storm's eye
Then hung out to dry
Left to starve and die
Like our lambs we lead to the slaughter
The killing seas begin the flood
While our fate bathes in their blood
Our future is forged and written in water

Red clouds of dust smother our mother earth
Much too late to count the cost of her worth
While our planet is taking its last breath
Our kiss steals her life by our Judas death

Zouma and Bro Get Their Kicks

The crack of the whip
Slashes the slave's back
See how the whip crack scars
The hot horse on the racetrack

A frit father too drunk to care
About his long-suffering wife
Who he hits so hard for so long
Once again she fears for her life
Then both batter the bruised baby
Then each pet gets kicked as yet
Users and losers and animal abusers
Boot-on-boot to a pet from her accuser

Compare the Zoumas' approach to animals
Shared by the brothers as common criminals

Our silence towards the one we shun
Because the uncaged truth remains
Cain caught in a tangled human skein
Points to all of us as none of us
Care enough for fugitives forever in chains

Zouma got his kicks holding his cat
Kick after kick of his scared pet cat
As his bro' filmed their sadistic abuse
Zouma held her as tight as a noose
No reason to hide their mocking pride
Yet it is the saddest sick sour spectacle
Given their ancestors were all manacled
Treated the same as the slave ship's rat

As the Zoumas inflicted hurt on their cat
Their vaunted power over a powerless cat
Their violence towards the screeching cat
While the victim's injuries still fester
Indulging in a history of mass-misery
The Zoumas betrayed their own ancestors
Standing chained in a naked frozen coffle
An uncaged truth defeats an abusers waffle
Past sadism shared by the bro's flummery
Strapped by Massa with a leather sliver
Before being sold down the soiled river
The frightened cat's fear makes her fur
Stand on end as she shakes and shivers
Zouma made such use of so much muscle
Kick-after-kick lands with so little tussle

Compare the Zoumas' approach to animals
Shared by the brothers as common criminals
When Zouma prepared to deliver
Another arrow of hate for his bro
To film as their own history quiver
Zouma got his seven-year-old son
To hold her so he could slap her
As she struggled trying to run
Their pet cat as a speciesist victim
Yet would shout from the rooftops
About themselves as racist victims
Zouma and his bro too crass to know
After all it is only a mangy Bengal cat
Zouma's a football hero how about that
How she feels is not part of their deal

Compare the Zoumas' approach to animals
Shared by the brothers as common criminals

Zouma stands tall at over six feet three
Easier to tower over a defenceless cat
To hold her so she cannot struggle free
At 15 stone he has too much to atone
His weight is sixty times that of a cat
So easy to score and easier using force
On a cat to inflict the maximum misery

If only the cat could get her revenge kicks
Like St Paul by kicking against the pricks
An epiphany so Zouma and his smiling bro
Feels the lasting power of the law's bricks
Where the stigma of a shared guilt sticks

Zuckerberg's Judas Goat

Zuckerberg boasts about how he digs
Eating his freshly-killed pig
And how he kills a goat
Because he is behind a moat
He figures it is fine to slit the throat
Of a pig and a goat
To end the life of an animal
Too weak to resist
The billionaire butcher's kiss
When the knife twists
In his clenched fist
Yet Zuckerberg is no sectarian
As his property is not pelf:
'I've basically become a vegetarian
Since the only meat I'm eating
Is from animals I've killed myself.'

Except the pig and goat
Cannot speak or reveal
But as both can feel
Neither can they reveal
Fear captured in their last squeal

Who says their last squeal
Was not telling Zuckerberg
Revisit the address at Gettysburg
Or death-row fear of Rosenberg
Zucker has ideas as cold as a fridge
That holds the pig
Before he holds her on his bridge
Though words float across his brow

Their meaning escape him for now
Given that his mind is never stationary
For a start he would be smart
To invest in a school dictionary
Zucker could look up 'vegetarian'
Then his mind might meet his heart

End to End

Searching for a dodo justice Soul

Law can show us what is real and what is not in relation to human affairs. Law has a power that is positive when it is used for the good of the community. Law is justice in action.

In *Nair v. Union of India* [2000] the judge in the Indian High Court delivered a judgment that promoted the end of the circus by using the principle of law with justice at its core. Narayana Kurup J. said:

'In conclusion, we hold that circus animals are being forced to perform unnatural tricks, are housed in cramped cages, subjected to fear, hunger, pain, not to mention the undignified way of life they have to live with no respite and the impugned notification has been issued in conformity with the changing scenario, values of human life, philosophy of the Constitution, prevailing conditions and the surrounding circumstances to prevent the infliction of unnecessary pain or suffering on animals. Though not homo sapiens, they are also beings entitled to dignified existences and humane treatment sans cruelty and torture.

Many believe that the lives of humans and animals are equally valuable and that their interest should count equally...

If humans are entitled to fundamental rights, why not animals?

In our considered opinion, legal rights shall not be the exclusive preserve of the humans which has to be extended beyond people thereby dismantling the thick legal wall with humans all on one side and all non-human animals on the other side.

While the law currently protects wildlife and endangered species from extinction, animals are denied rights, an anachronism which must necessarily change.'

Kurup is right. Justice is indivisible. There is no reason why animals should be denied the protection of the mantle of law and indeed every reason for it to apply to them. Wherever they are harmed by us and suffer from abuse they are 'entitled' to be protected. A law that fails to protect animals from us is edentulous.

Law protects the underdog. Animals have always been our underdogs' underdog yet are denied legal protection from us when we decide to deliberately cause them "necessary suffering". Whatever we gain in material terms will prove how short-sighted we are as our loss will be calculated by the scales of blind justice. A world without animals would be a world without vision: for in our failure to see what matters dung beetles are the lodestar of our law.

How long can we fail to see that animals should be respected by being granted 'rights'? Who could take Descartes seriously when he was an abusive mendacious dyed-in-the-wool vivisectionist? He was the ancestor of Pavlov who tortured dogs for fun. Then when they barked through fear while being literally scared to death, their howls irritated Pavlov. His solution was to remove their voice box so he could not hear the torturous sounds which assaulted his ears. Pavlov was such a sensitive scientist he could not bear the hear the sounds of the animals' suffering he had deliberately caused. Pavlov conveniently found solace in the sound of silence as he then did not have any reminder of his calculated violence. Yet from abattoirs to zoos, is he any less than our own reflection?

Being human with rights means you are entitled to be treated with respect and rectitude and your claim and you receive the dignity you deserve. Then whatever the result or verdict the judge and jury deliver, all those affected can rest easy in the belief that justice has been done. However it is quite another thing altogether when you are designated to be a thing as a matter of law. Then because you are voiceless you remain outside the law. That is no less than justice denied because those in power have a power over you as the powerless. Your fortune and future then forever depends upon their sense of innate fairness as your right to remain alive or otherwise does not exist. As a result of that position and reasoning the Whanganui River was granted 'a legal personality' in New Zealand in 2017 after a 140-year battle. Why is the blood of an animal less worthy legally than the silver flow of a river?

Our relationship with animals was considered in *R. v. Menard* [1978] by the Quebec Court of Appeal where Lamer JA. said:

'On the other hand, the animal is inferior to man, and takes its place within a hierarchy which is the hierarchy of animals, and above all is part of nature with all its "racial and natural" selections. The animal is subordinate to nature and to man. It will often be in the interests of man to kill and mutilate wild or domestic animals, to subjugate them and, to this end, to tame them with all the painful consequence this may entail for them and, if they are too old, or too numerous, or abandoned, to kill them.'

This explanation denies rights to animals and denotes our duties towards them when it is considered necessary to control human behaviour. So in the legal sense the animal as a defendant is tried by a human prosecutor and a human judge and jury. The animal has neither a defence counsel nor a defence. Nor can the animal ever have a defence. For the crime the animal has committed is solely being born and the figurative trial is a denial of natural justice.

The words used by Lamer underline the reasons why animals are exploited. So there was no possible doubt about it he explained in detail that animals are in 'our world' and so any protection given to them is a result of 'The responsibilities that we impose on ourselves as their masters.' His judgment was no less than legal speciesism based on the historical misguided morals of Aristotle.

We have moved from being anthropomorphic to anthropo-centric by using our might to prove we are right. If we end up with a world without bees that would be a symbol our law as our symbol of morality has failed. While such a world sounds extreme it is now in our vision.

Most human beings now have 'rights' because they are human beings. Rights extend to all within the category of homo sapiens. That is our limit. Therefore the same practice may be legal or illegal according to the victim and the profit to us.

Our failure to protect animals from us is a Pyhrric victory for profit over ethics where the weak perish on the altar of our avarice. We squander the lives of animals for a monetary mirage when we should be staring into a mirror of our own morality. Our decision depends as much on our vision as on our understanding of law. For as with the soul of a single cow, it is a truth both rare and raw that feral justice is the soul of our common law. A belief in the religious sense of our superiority has permeated the sinews of our law. It is why the idea that we have a soul whilst animals do not has fixed our superiority and the consequent inferiority of animals.

Yet the notion is based on a notion that has no validity at all. It is naked prejudice that enables us to practise abuse because our strength overpowers their birthmark curse of being born an animal. Reza Aslan in *God: A Human History of Religion* [2018] details the true position:

'Where did the idea of the soul come from?

The truthful answer is we don't know...It is the result of something far more primal and difficult to explain: our ingrained, intuitive, and wholly experiential belief that we are, whatever else we are, embodied souls.

Our quest in the following chapters is neither to prove nor to disprove the existence of the soul (there is no proof either way).'

Clarence Darrow in *Verdicts Out of Court* [1963] analysed the myth of the soul:

'It is impossible to draw the line between inorganic matter and the simpler forms of plant life, and equally impossible to draw the line between plant life and animal life, or between other forms of animal life and what we human beings are pleased to call the highest form. If the thing which we call "life" is itself the soul, then cows have souls; and, in the very nature of things, we must allow souls to all forms of life and to inorganic matter as well.'

Aslan and Darrow are right. Our problem in promoting prejudice towards animals by law is self-engendered. It has neither sense nor sensibility on its side because it is not derived from a logical base. The result stems from a caveman philosophy and ends in a dodo justice. We gain by the pain inflicted on an innocent unwilling victim. That is inhumane and unethical. Ultimately the fate of animals and us is inextricably linked. In the mystery of living our destinies are interdependent and interrelated and interwoven. That self-evident truth should be reflected in our mirror of morality for law is the universal language of natural justice.

When Salt's classic work, *Animals' Rights*, was reviewed by a Victorian feminist, Edith Ward, she stated in the aptly-named *Shafts* [1892], 'the case for the animal is the case of the woman. What [is] more likely to impress mankind with the necessity of justice for women than the awakening of the idea that justice was the right of even an ox or a sheep?'

Isonomy has no meaning or purpose if equality applies to humans alone. Philosophical discussions about rights are as valueless as verbal smoke-rings fading into thin air unless and until animals possess a defined legal status. If it is right that we can assume a superior role over animals and then treat or ill-treat them accordingly, then the law is wrong. Animals are entitled by virtue of being alive and sentient to the reciprocal protection within the mantle of law. It is not that they breathe the same air as us that matters, but that they breathe to have life. Justice for animals is rooted in their very existence. It is not a question of our self-serving excuse of it being life and life only, for it is   death and death only.

Narayana Kurup J. in the *Balakrishnan Case* [2000] discerned our lawful negativity towards animals. His evaluation was and remains a universal lodestone judgment:

'Legal rights shall not be the exclusive preserve of the humans which has to be extended beyond people thereby dismantling the thick legal wall with humans all on one side and all non-human animals on the other side...animals are denied rights, an anachronism which must necessarily change.'

That wall is our equivalent of the Berlin Wall which denied the people behind it freedom and justice. Unlike that demolished wall, the one we have constructed between animals and us applies injustice throughout the world. The legal wall we have constructed between animals and us is built with bricks of natural injustice.

English Law is impotent in failing to respect animals' rights. When our gain is measured by the pain inflicted on a vulnerable victim, it is unethical to continue the practice.

Animals need to be freed from our legal yoke. Natural justice as the quintessence of law must recognise the self-evident truth we are all animals-in-law. A legal system that fails to protect vulnerable victims thereby promotes the letter and spirit of injustice. In facing that charge English Law provides the evidence to prove itself 'Guilty'.

Zwischenzug proves a check-rein move

The camel's back cracked by the man of straw
Yet nothing was hidden from vision nor the law
The monkey on the camel is a pot-luck crook
Until a sniper proudly cocks his zumbooruk

Caught across zugzwang's profit plus its loss
Hooked on the rusty shattered sign of Thanatos
Lies disguised as truth in a human intercross
Fate's forged fortune versus the last lone albatross

A final move proves the price of a zwischenzug
A slow death by ecocide as our choice of drug
A lesson too late to learn whether gold or dross
As trust soon dies under a black moon's wounded eyes
Our guilt traded for a Janus kissed double-cross
Blindfold clouds concealed an anarchist albatross

Index

The titles and first lines of the poems and the prose

Advocate

Noël Sweeney is a practising barrister who specializes in criminal law and human rights and animal law. He has lectured and written on all those subjects including the legal role and status of animals. Sweeney has presented his poems and songs on animal rights in bars and beneath stars. While he is not prone to follow any particular person or creed, he favours those who pursue the cause of justice for those unable to do so because they are branded by birth as victims of our prejudice.

Sweeney does not wish animals were empowered over people, but merely possess the power to determine and live their own lives. For the only valid voice animals can own is the sound of justice delivered by the pure core of law.

While he has no heroes in or out of the law, Sweeney has a defined admiration for Kurt Westergaard who drew the cartoon reprinted in the Charlie Hebdo magazine. Westergaard was neither cowed nor impressed by threats from arrogated people driven by religious zealotry. He wished to be remembered as 'the one who struck a blow for the freedom of expression.' His memory sits side-by-side with the perfervid activist stride of the teenage rebel, the soul-tossed eyed Claudette Colvin.

Sweeney still misses Cyril the squirrel who used to regularly visit and entertain people with his natural acrobatics. Although there are about a quarter of a million red squirrels and two-and-half million grey ones, to each one their life matters. When Cyril and any other squirrel is killed in jest, like the rest of us, rest assured he dies in earnest.